Around the Clock

A Play

by Nick Hall

A SAMUEL FRENCH ACTING EDITION

FOUNDED 1830

SAMUELFRENCH.COM

ISBN   978-0-573-62990-7   Printed   in   U.S.A.   #3747

MUSIC USE NOTE

IMPORTANT BILLING AND CREDIT REQUIREMENTS

CHARACTERS

Polly Harrison

Kendall Bornot

Lacey Reed

Jessica Sheridan

Prudence Alvarez

Gillian Sheridan

SETTING

Living room of a suburban house in north Florida

Act I
Midday, mid-week

Act II
A week later

ACT I

(The setting is the living room of a large suburban house. It shows signs of upscale affluence without being too fussy or ornate. There is a door [probably a swing door] to the kitchen areas Down Left. There is a console table against Left wall upstage of that door. In the rear, Upstage, wall of the room is a large entry, raised one or two steps. From here, Offstage Right is the front door, Offstage Left leads to the rest of the house. In the Up Right corner of he room is a decorative folding-screen. In the Right wall there is a large window, probably with sheer drapes or blinds, as a view is not needed. Against the Right wall downstage of the window is a small telephone table or stand, beside it a straight-backed chair. There is a couch Left of Center, angled to Center. Behind it a narrow console table. In front of the sofa is a hassock or padded stool, usable as a coffee table. Left of Center is a matching armchair with a small occasional table to the Left of it. Apart from any other decorations there may be, in the Up Left corner, hanging against the rear wall is a stuffed fish mounted on a plaque. This may be a little incongruous. The overall impression should be attractive.

POLLY HARRISON enters from the kitchen, carrying five ashtrays and a duster. She is middle-aged, a little flustered and dressed for cleaning, possibly sweat pants and a large faded Hawaiian shirt. She is wiping the ashtrays as she comes in. She flicks the console table, Left, with the duster and places an ashtray, crosses and repeats at the armchair table. Crosses behind couch to put one on that table.

KENDALL BORNOT enters from the rest of the house Up Center. She is young and well dressed, almost suitable for business. POLLY does not notice her and continues with the ashtrays and dusting.)

KENDALL. What time is it?

POLLY. *(Still holding duster and a couple of ashtrays looks awkwardly at her watch.)* Nearly twelve o'clock. But this is unreliable. It may be fast.

KENDALL. *(Who has crossed to the Left console table and picked up the ashtray. She will follow in POLLY's footsteps picking up all the ashtrays.)* Did you vacuum?

POLLY. Yes, earlier, while you were out jogging.

KENDALL. Did you exercise? You should exercise, you know.

POLLY. No, I didn't exercise. I did the bedrooms and the bathrooms and the kitchen, vacuumed here. And the cooking, of course.

KENDALL. The food's ready?

POLLY. *(Who has put ashtrays on the phone table and the hassock in front of the sofa.)* Yes, it's all ready, except for the crab thing; that has to be warmed up at the last minute. I wish you'd let me do those barbeque beef ribs. Everybody loves them; some of them expect them.

KENDALL. *(Who has brought all the ashtrays to POLLY at Center.)* No red meat. *(Picks up the last ashtray and hands it to POLLY.)* And no smoking, remember.

POLLY. *(Taking ashtrays.)* Yes, but with people coming. Guests. And some of them do. Gillian does.

KENDALL. No smoking.

POLLY. *(Heading to kitchen with ashtrays.)* Well, if you say so, but I'm not sure Gillian can talk without a cigarette in her hand. And you know how ....

(The phone rings. POLLY exits to kitchen. KENDALL goes to phone.)

KENDALL. *(One phone.)* Hello.... Oh, hello, Mary, I'm Kendall.... Oh, I'm sorry to hear that. What a pity. Yes, of course, close tc home.... Mary, there's the other line. Can you hold a second? *(Punches button.)* Hello.... Yes, yes it is. Oh, good, we'd love to have you. Yes, next Thursday, seven-thirty, here. You have the address? Great. The group is Home Again, Home Again.... No, you said Home Again. And it's not Home Again; it's Home Again, Home Again.... Because that's the name—you have to say it twice.... Well, great, and remember Caring, Sharing and Self-Esteem. Bye.

(KENDALL hangs up.
During the second call POLLY enters from the kitchen carrying a tray with an ice bucket with a champagne bottle in it, orange juice, Bloody Mary mix, vodka and a container of celery stalks. She is heading for the drinks console Left. KENDALL turns.)

KENDALL. That was .... *(Registers drinks.)* What is that? What do you think you are doing?
POLLY. Who, well, it's just Bloody Marys and Mimosas. And in case somebody wants a screwdriver.
KENDALL. No alcohol.
POLLY. Some of them like a drink at lunchtime.
KENDALL. No alcohol. Absolutely no alcohol. You're not going to wear that, are you?
POLLY. *(Looking at self.)* What, this? Oh, no I'm going to change in a minute.
KENDALL. Now who's coming?
POLLY. Well, Jessica and Gillian, of course ...
KENDALL. ... the dinosaurs ...
POLLY. ... and somebody I don't know from the Community College, I'm not sure why. And somebody who's a friend of .... *(The doorbell rings.)* Good Lord, I haven't changed.
KENDALL. Will you get that.
POLLY. You know, I don't think my watch is fast.

(The doorbell rings.)

KENDALL. Mother, will you get that.
POLLY. *(Who is still holding the drinks tray.)* Yes, dear.

(POLLY turns and starts for the door.)

KENDALL. Mother, the drinks. You're holding the drinks.
POLLY. Maybe they'll want one.
KENDALL. *(Taking tray.)* Well, they can't have one. *(Taking tray.)* I'll do this; you do that.

(KENDALL exits with tray to the kitchen.)

POLLY. *(Going to front door.)* I wish I'd changed. *(Opens door to LACEY.)* Hello, there.
LACEY. *(Young, dress slightly funky, perhaps a leotard with a fringed shawl tied around the waist, carrying a sports bottle.)* Good morning, afternoon, whatever.
POLLY. *(Ushering her in.)* You know, I knew this *(means her watch)* was unreliable and I thought it was fast. But it's not fast, is it? Just unreliable. But come in, come in. You must be a friend of Mary's.
LACEY. Mary who?
POLLY. Or maybe not. Would you like a drink? Oh, sorry, you can't have one. Well, you could have an orange juice, but no vodka in it. So it wouldn't be a screwdriver. It would be an orange juice.
KENDALL. *(Entering from kitchen, carrying the tray on which are some glasses, orange juice and a carafe of water.)* Hello, there. *(Setting down tray.)* Drink? I'm sorry it's not freshly squeezed, but this is pure, spring water.
LACEY. *(Raising her bottle.)* No thanks. Mrs. Harrison?
KENDALL. No, I'm Kendall. Kendall Bornot, her daughter. This is my mother, Mrs. Harrison. Polly Harrison.
LACEY. Pleased to meet you.
POLLY. I was going to change.

LACEY. Lacey Welsh. I'm from the college. Racy Lacey here to play.

POLLY. What do you teach?

LACEY. Theatre. Acting.

KENDALL. Is that how you got roped into this?

LACEY. I guess. The chair of the department said I should get involved in the community. It would help me get tenure. I'm just an instructor; I need tenure. To pay the rent.

POLLY. Of course, you do.

LACEY. And I've heard about you: You're the ladies who're putting on the play about a clock. Tell me about the clock.

POLLY. It's very pretty.

LACEY. Oh, I thought ...

POLLY. *(Enthusiastically.)* It's for the new shopping mall. Mary Steadman's husband Dan is building a new shopping mall—but a very nice one, right downtown, open-air, pedestrian, cobblestones. And anyway, Mary was in Germany and she found this clock-tower that she could buy for the mall; and she did. Buy it.

LACEY. What kind of clock is this?

POLLY. Very pretty. I've got some pictures.

KENDALL. It's a huge clock-tower, three stories tall with mechanical moving figures. Late medieval. A Glockenspiel. They're bringing it over piece by piece.

LACEY. Wow, that must cost a fortune.

KENDALL. Well, Mary has a fortune. And friends with fortunes: Gillian and Jessica.

LACEY. And we're here because ...?

POLLY. Because Mary got some of us girls together ....

KENDALL. *(Interrupting sharply.)* Mother! You are not girls.

POLLY. Well, I know, dear. It's just something I say.

KENDALL. *(To LACEY.)* Hopeless.

POLLY. Mary got us together to raise interest and support in the town. A community, civic sort of thing. I mean, the clock could become a tourist attraction. So we decided to do a presentation, a pageant really of the figures on the clock. You know, the figures move; they come in and out and go all around. We're doing it at the next meeting of the Chamber of Commerce. And it's open to the public. We'd love you to come.

KENDALL. *(Grimly patient.)* She's going to be in it.

POLLY. Oh, that's right. Well, we're very glad to have you. If it's successful, we're going to go on to the Kiwanis and then the Elks and who knows where it will all end.

LACEY. What sort of figures?

POLLY. Very pretty. There's this saint and an angel and a knight in armor.

LACEY. My kinda guy.

POLLY. Oh, and an evil queen, and what else, dear?

KENDALL. Death. With a scythe.

POLLY. They're life-sized figures. So we're all going to dress up like them and do the movements. *(Pause—the other two don't respond.)* Well, there'll be music, you know. Oomh pah pah. *(Pause.)* And Mary's going to do some narration to tell the story.

LACEY. *(To KENDALL.)* Wow, this must be sold out already.

KENDALL. There are families camping on the sidewalk outside the Chamber of Commerce.

POLLY. You can laugh, but I think it's a great idea. I'm working up a cheer for us. *(Starting off to kitchen.)* I've got some pictures. Mary's got a video, but I've got pictures. I'll show you and then you'll get in the spirit of the thing. Be right back.

(POLLY exits kitchen.)

LACEY. I can't believe I'm here doing this.

KENDALL. I'm here because I live here; not much choice.

LACEY. You still live at home?

KENDALL. Not really. I just moved back. I got a divorce.

LACEY. Obviously, you didn't get the house?

KENDALL. We didn't have one, we rented, but I got everything else.

LACEY. Way to go. And speaking of men, which I often am, are there any involved in this clock thing?

KENDALL. No, it's all women.

LACEY. A chick flick. Are they all rich?

KENDALL. Well, let's see Gillian is—she made hers in software with Henry. And Jessica—she married it. And Mary inherited it. Mary and Gillian go way back with Mother. But we're definitely not rich now, we sort of nearly were, but then the bubble burst and Father died and we're lucky the house is paid for. *(Gesturing house.)* My inheritance.

LACEY. Pretty nice.

KENDALL. Pretty valuable. Mother thought of selling it. Betty Wilson wants it already. But I think I've put a stop to that. There's even been talk of a reverse mortgage.

LACEY. What's that?

KENDALL. It's how they prove they *can* take it with them. Thank Heavens she's too young.

POLLY. *(Entering from the kitchen and crossing quickly up to rest of house.)* They're not in the kitchen. Why did I think they were in the kitchen? Be right back.

(POLLY exits to rest of the house.)

KENDALL. *(Staring after POLLY.)* But I think I'm needed here.

LACEY. So if we're all women, who's going to play the knight in shining armor?

KENDALL. One of us.

LACEY. Please. I've got some guys in my night class. I have this Latin guy. He could play a knight. Magnificently. You know, for extra credit.

KENDALL. You give a lot of extra credit?

LACEY. To the right guy, I do. And, girlfriend, Nando is the right guy.

KENDALL. Nando?

LACEY. Short for Fernando. Fernando Alvarez—tall, dark and take-your-shirt-off. I think he should quit his job and go into acting full time. I think I could help him. I'm gonna help him. And Racy Lacey always gets her man.

(The doorbell rings.)

KENDALL. Excuse me. *(Going to front door.)* Mother's still in the back; I'll get it. *(Opens the doors.)* Oh, hello, Jessica.

JESSICA. Hello, Kendall. *(Coming into the room. JESSICA is wearing a Tyrolean hat and a complete lederhosen outfit authentic in every detail, except for the stiletto heels.)* Well, darlings, I've got butterflies in my stomach, stage fright, and opening night nerves. But you know me—I'm a trouper. I'm ready to go on again.

KENDALL. Jessica was almost in show business once.

LACEY. Hi.

KENDALL. This is Lacey....

LACEY. Racy Lacey from the college.

KENDALL. And this is Jessica Sheridan, friend of Mother's.

JESSICA. How d'you do?

LACEY. *(Simultaneously.)* Pleased to meet you.

KENDALL. Jessica, what are you wearing?

JESSICA. Lederhosen. From Germany.

KENDALL. Why?

JESSICA. Well, it's a German clock, isn't it? I'm getting into character. And anyway, I phoned Mary and she said wear something suitable. So is she here yet?

KENDALL. Who?

JESSICA. Gillian. The dreaded Gillian is back in town after a long blissful absence.

LACEY. Why dreaded?

JESSICA. You don't want to know; there's history there. *(No animus.)* Terrible woman—she drinks, smokes, swears, gambles.

KENDALL. *(To JESSICA.)* So do you?

JESSICA. I don't gamble. And I only swear occasionally, mostly at Henry behind his back.

KENDALL. *(Interrupting.)* Jessica is married to Henry— Gillian's ex-husband.

JESSICA. Excuse me, Kendall, but that was my line. My life: my line.

KENDALL. Sorry, but I got us there faster. With less histrionics.

JESSICA. Well, where's Polly?

KENDALL. She's looking for some pictures of the clock.

JESSICA. Did she make the ribs?

KENDALL. No red meat.

JESSICA. Oh, dear. Well, Racy ....

LACEY. Lacey.

JESSICA. Lacey. So you're from the college. What do you do there?

LACEY. I'm an instructor; Speech and Drama.

JESSICA. No! What do you teach? I was in the theater before I met Henry. I gave up the theater for Henry.

KENDALL. I've only got two classes right now. Intro to Speech and Phonetics, and Acting for the Non-Actor.

JESSICA. What's that?

LACEY. We're using acting as a problem-solving tool for the business community in its relationship with the public. The liberating aspects of rehearsal and performance a psychosocial terrain for the development of techniques that permit not just presentation to, but also interaction with, and consequently co-optation of the targeted clients.

JESSICA. I'm guessing no Neil Simon.

LACEY. Well, that's what it says in the catalogue. But it's good for public relations people, so companies enroll their employees and we get a lot more young guys than usual.

JESSICA. I've forgotten, what do you do, Kendall?

KENDALL. I'm Vice President of SPOUTS. The Society for the

Prevention Of Undesirable Traits. You know, we were lobbying for the digital removal of cigarettes from Humphrey Bogart movies, and we were going to file an amicus brief in the lawsuit against Oreo Cookies, unfortunately the suit was dropped. Anyway, we're a non-profit organization.

JESSICA. I'll bet you are.

KENDALL. Well, actually, at the moment I'm not with them. Since the divorce. But it's just as well, because I'm really busy. I'm starting my own new support group. It's called Home Again, Home Again. It's for adult children returning home. There's lots of issues; we're going to meet here Thursday evenings. And I've got Tai Chi lessons and pottery class. I'm a soldier in the army of the War on Violence. And then there's Mother. I need time for Mother.

JESSICA. What do you mean? What about Polly? Where is she? Is she ill?

KENDALL. No, no, nothing like that. But you must have noticed that lately she's a little, well, unfocussed. She's flustered. You know, since Father died.

JESSICA. I didn't notice. She's very active. She still works parttime at the Library, doesn't she?

KENDALL. Yes, yes. I didn't mean anything major. It's just I'd like to keep an eye on her. I'm already working on her diet.

LACEY. Any guys coming Home Again, Home Again?

KENDALL. Well, it's open to everyone. Every race, religion, sexual ....

JESSICA. *(Interrupting.)* I wouldn't count on a lot of men, Lacey.

POLLY. *(Entering hurriedly UC with some loose photos.)* You know, they weren't in my desk after all. I was sure they were, but they weren't. They were in the laundry room. Which was the last place I looked ....

KENDALL. *(Quietly to JESSICA.)* See.

POLLY. ... Jessica!

JESSICA. *(Simultaneously.)* Polly.

(Quick embrace.)

POLLY. I'm so sorry, I was going to change. *(Registers leder-hosen.)* Are you going to change?
JESSICA. I did. It's German.
POLLY. Foreigners are funny that way, aren't they?
KENDALL. *(Appalled.)* Mother!
POLLY. How's everything? How are the children?
JESSICA. They're great. They're at Grandma's this week. But you know the kids are always great; it's Henry that takes the effort ....
LACEY. *(To KENDALL.)* Henry is ...?
KENDALL. Jessica's current; Gillian's ex.
JESSICA. Listen, Polly, I was taking Atilla to the vets to see if that scratching was normal, and I had to pick up Diana's dress on the way and I ran into the Wilsons. Betty Wilson will pay top dollar for this house. Top dollar. But how are you? Are you okay? You look ....
POLLY. It's just because I didn't get a chance to change. I'm fine, same as always. I've got some pictures of the clock for Lacey. *(The doorbell rings.)* That's probably Mary or Gillian. I'll get it. *(Hands photos to LACEY as she goes.)* Help Lacey with the pictures. They're not too clear. But you can tell it's very pretty. *(POLLY opens the door to PRUDENCE ALVAREZ, twenties, wearing a maternity dress, pregnant, showing but not hugely. She carries a folder of loose papers.)* Hello, there. Now you must be Mary's friend. I'm Polly Harrison. Come in, come in.
PRUDENCE. *(Entering, simultaneously.)* Hello. Yes, I am. I'm Prudence. Prudence Alvarez. Lovely house.
POLLY. Thank you. It's more house than we ever needed, but that's what people were doing then, and my husband and daughter wanted it. Everybody, this is Prudence, a friend of Mary's.
LACEY. *(Simultaneously.)* Hi, there.
KENDALL. *(Simultaneously.)* Hello.
JESSICA. *(Simultaneously.)* Oh, hello, I've heard so much about you from the Steadmans. You're the public accountant; the tax lady?

PRUDENCE. Yes. I'm working from home these days.

POLLY. Sit down, dear, sit down. Would you like something to drink?

PRUDENCE. No, I'm fine thank you.

POLLY. I've left the door open for Mary and Gillian

PRUDENCE. Mary's not coming; didn't you know? She said she phoned.

KENDALL. Oh, that's right! She did phone. I forgot.

PRUDENCE. Some sort of stomach thing.

POLLY. But then we can't go on, can we? Mary is the clock. She bought it. She's the one who knows how the figures move. And she was going to be in it, too—one of the figures.

PRUDENCE. It's okay. She said just go on without her. *(Indicating papers.)* She sent instructions, diagrams. She said just work around her and she'll be here next time.

KENDALL. Then can we get started.

POLLY. We've two people missing.

LACEY. Who are these people—figures?

PRUDENCE. I've got a list here, and the story and stuff.

KENDALL. Then let's have it. Read it.

PRUDENCE. *(Hesitant.)* Well I, ... the thing is, I ....

JESSICA. I'll do it....

(JESSICA takes papers.)

POLLY. Yes, Jessica, you do it. Okay, girls, gather round.

KENDALL. Mother, we are not girls!

LACEY. Oh, I think I am.

(Everybody, except JESSICA, is seated or perched somewhere.)

JESSICA. *(Standing.)* Listen. *(Reading, rather as if to children.)* "Once upon a time in olden days in a Barbarian Kingdom ruled by Evil Pagan Queen Gundra, lived a pure and virtuous Christian maiden named Ermintrude.

LACEY. Well, you'd have to be pure with a name like that.

JESSICA. "Now Evil Pagan Queen Gundra hated Ermintrude because she was beautiful and good. Ermintrude gathered flowers for the church and was loved from afar by a noble Christian knight. But Evil Pagan Queen Gundra was herself in love with the noble Christian knight, who loved only Ermintrude. So Evil Pagan Queen Gundra dragged Ermintrude away to her castle. And summoned Death. Then Evil Pagan Queen ...

KENDALL. For Heaven's sakes, don't say Evil Pagan Queen whosit, again.

JESSICA. *(Irked.)* Listen, I didn't write this stuff. *(Resumes, deliberately.)* "And *Gundra* had Death bind Ermintrude in a sack and throw her into the river to drown. And all the simple good people of the Kingdom wept.

POLLY. But the simple, good people of the Kingdom aren't really moving figures. They're just carved on the clock. Not moving.

JESSICA. She's in the sack, in the river, drowning. "When lo, a heavenly angel appeared and Ermintrude was saved, and became a holy nun.

LACEY. If you call that being saved.

JESSICA. "But Death would not return without a victim. And she took *(Deliberately.)* Evil Pagan Queen Gundra with him. To her doom." *(Lowering papers.)* There you are.

PRUDENCE. Very good. It sounds like fun.

KENDALL. We can't do it. In fact, they shouldn't build the clock. It's religious; it's overt, flagrant, public Christianity. It might offend somebody.

(GILLIAN SHERIDAN enters UC. Crisp tan slacks, crisp white shirt. The others do not notice.)

POLLY. Who? Pagans? There aren't any pagans around here.

LACEY. You'd be surprised.

PRUDENCE. I think she means Muslims, Jews, Wiccans.

POLLY. What are Wiccans, dear?

KENDALL. It should be an inclusive, multicultural clock.

JESSICA. It's just a clock, for Heaven's sake. It's a clock.

KENDALL. Well, I just don't think it's right. It's exactly that type of thoughtless, cavalier attitude that ....

GILLIAN. *(Crossing down into room.)* You know, it's a funny thing about Fifteenth Century Germany; they didn't build a lot of multicultural clocks.

POLLY. *(Pleased.)* Gillian.

GILLIAN. And anyway, it's probably a Christian legend grafted onto a pre-Christian folk tale that incorporated traces of classical Greek mythology, which should be multicultural enough for most people. *(Having taken in JESSICA's outfit.)* On the other hand, Jessica, it's not a cuckoo clock.

JESSICA. Oh, well, this is German.

GILLIAN. It's also male. It's what German men wear. Women wear the Dirndl.

JESSICA. What's that?

GILLIAN. A sort of flouncy, bouncy peasant thing. Perfect for you.

POLLY. Gillian, you're late.

GILLIAN. Good. I already know the exposition.

POLLY. You don't know Lacey; she's from the college because she needs tenure. *(LACEY and GILLIAN smile and semi-nod.)* I was going to change.

GILLIAN. *(Looking pointedly at JESSICA.)* Good thing you didn't.

LACEY. Okay, let's cast this thing. Who wants to play what?

JESSICA. Well, I want to play Saint Ermintrude; she's got costume changes.

PRUDENCE. Really, Ermintrude is three different figures on the clock. You know the virtuous maiden, drowning in the sack, and the holy Saint. Three parts.

JESSICA. Oh, no costume changes.

LACEY. *(Snide.)* Bummer.

JESSICA. Well, I still want to play Ermintrude. She's the lead.

POLLY. Jessica, don't you think for Saint Ermintrude we need someone ... well ... more ....

JESSICA. Saintly? I can do saintly.

GILLIAN. Younger.

JESSICA. I can do ....

GILLIAN. *(Firmly.)* Much younger.

POLLY. Lacey, dear, you're young, why don't you play Ermintrude. The third one; the holy saint.

LACEY. Okay. But it's gonna be an enormous stretch.

PRUDENCE. And now we need a virtuous maiden.

GILLIAN. Well, Kendall, you're oozing goodness from every pore. You could play Ermintrude gathering flowers.

KENDALL. *(Insincere.)* Thank you, Gillian.

PRUDENCE. And there's still another Ermintrude—tied up in the sack.

GILLIAN. Jessica.

JESSICA. *(Simultaneously.)* Gillian. *(Beat.)* I don't want to be tied up in a sack. Prudence is young.

POLLY. Prudence is pregnant; we can't tie her up in a sack.

LACEY. Listen, if we're one person short, why don't we just drag the sack around with us.

POLLY. We could do that today, but eventually there'll have to be someone in the sack, because of the movements—all the figures have movements.

PRUDENCE. Nearly all of them.

LACEY. What short of movements?

POLLY. Oh, cute. Very cute movements. Prudence, dear, why don't you play the Angel. It's not a strenuous part.

PRUDENCE. Yes, okay.

KENDALL. We need a knight in armor.

LACEY. If we're one short, I have a student who could play the knight.

GILLIAN. Jessica? A knight in shining armor?

JESSICA. Is that a big part.

PRUDENCE. It's about as big as they get on a clock.

KENDALL. And then there's Evil Pagan Queen Gundra.

JESSICA. *(Too sweetly.)* Gillian?

GILLIAN. Fine by me, provided Kendall doesn't object to typecasting.

KENDALL. No, no, I certainly think you can play an Evil Pagan Queen.

JESSICA. You may win an award for it.

LACEY. That's it then. We're all cast.

PRUDENCE. No, there's one left.

LACEY. Who hasn't got a part?

GILLIAN. Polly.

KENDALL. Well, Mother, I guess you're Death.

JESSICA. Shall I direct, I was in the theater?

GILLIAN. Jessica, I'm not sure that wearing fishnet stockings and sequins twice a night counts as 'in the theater'.

(Peeved, JESSICA turns away and starts looking through the photos.)

LACEY. I could do it; I mean I teach theater; I know blocking. Maybe we could do it as a medieval mystery play or a Commedia piece. And anyway, you have to have someone with an overall vision. Someone with a complete grasp of the text who can plumb the depths and answer the really big, probing questions.

JESSICA. What are all these fish?

POLLY. From the river. After she was saved, Ermintrude always distributed fish to the poor. And she helped the blind and the crippled.

KENDALL. *(Automatically.)* Physically challenged.

LACEY. *(Overlapping, automatically.)* Visually impaired.

PRUDENCE. *(To LACEY.)* You teach at the college? *(LACEY smiles and nods.)* I think my husband's in your evening class. Nando.

LACEY. Nando?

PRUDENCE. Short for Fernando. Fernando Alvarez.

LACEY. Fernando Alvarez? Yes, I think he is. I'll check.

PRUDENCE. He really likes it. He asked me if he should become an actor. Of course, he was only joking.

LACEY. *(Smiles.)* Of course.

(Though she hears the above, KENDALL does not react.)

POLLY. Sounds very silly to me, I mean he has that nice position with Dan and Mary. Gillian, do you think you can get the Mayor to come? Maybe the Sheriff?

GILLIAN. They're coming. I did it already. And the Dean from the college and some local media.

POLLY. Bless you.

JESSICA. Where are we going to do it, Polly? Here?

POLLY. Yes, if that's okay.

LACEY. Sure. *(LACEY has notes and walks this out; defining their clock playing area as Down Center in front of the furniture. PRUDENCE also has a set of notes.)* Look, imagine the clock face is here. And there's an archway entrance here on the right....

PRUDENCE. That's the left.

LACEY. Stage Right. And another one her on the left.

PRUDENCE. Stage left?

LACEY. Right.

POLLY. I'll move this *(hassock in front of sofa)* out of the way.

(POLLY does so.)

LACEY. Let's put something to mark the arches. *(Goes to straight-backed chair Down Right.)* Here, we can use this for one of them. *(Sets chair, facing upstage, Downstage Right of Center.)* And then we can use ....

GILLIAN. We can use this *(small table beside armchair)* for the other side. *(Moves it into position Downstage Left of Center.)* There we are.

LACEY. So here *(Indicating Right of straight-backed chair.)* is the right archway; and over here *(Left of table.)* is the left archway.
PRUDENCE. And what's all this here?

(PRUDENCE is indicating space between, Down Center.)

POLLY. *(To PRUDENCE.)* Usually there's a pretty Persian carpet there, but it's at the cleaners.
LACEY. Okay, let's get it straight. *(DC, facing Upstage.)* There is the face of the clock. The bottom of the face of a big, really big clock. There are archway entrances on either side, which we've marked. And here *(Where she is standing, extreme Down Center. As she says this she turns around in place, indicating:)* is the platform where the figures move. *(To PRUDENCE.)* That's right, isn't it?
PRUDENCE. Yes, I think so.
LACEY. Okay, everybody ready?
GILLIAN. Yes.
JESSICA. *(Simultaneously.)* I am.
KENDALL. *(Simultaneously.)* Yes.
LACEY. Okay, the first figure to come out is Saint Ermintrude. *(No one moves.)* Saint Ermintrude. *(Realizes.)* Oh, that's me.

(LACEY starts to move.)

PRUDENCE. No, it's the other Ermintrude. Before she was a saint.
KENDALL. Me. Me. Virtuous maiden. Her I am.

(KENDALL moves DC.)

LACEY. Okay, you have to come on from the left archway and go Center.
KENDALL. *(Moving Left.)* This left?
LACEY. That left. *(As KENDALL "enters" and moves Center.)* Through the archway ... and curve round ... and moves Center ... and

stops. Good.

(Pause as KENDALL stands awkwardly Center.)

LACEY. *(Looking at notes.)* And the next figure is ....

PRUDENCE. EPQG.

POLLY. What?

PRUDENCE. Evil Pagan Queen Gundra.

GILLIAN. From which side?

LACEY. Stage Right entrance.

GILLIAN. *(Moving there.)* Okay. Ready.

LACEY. *(Slowly, as GILLIAN executes it.)* And moves Center. Good. And pauses.

GILLIAN. *(To KENDALL.)* Well, here we are; Vice and Virtue, face to face.

LACEY. ... and continues round and exits Stage Right. *(Which GILLIAN does.)* Good.

POLLY. Well done, Gillian.

LACEY. And now it's the knight in shining armor.

JESSICA. Me.

PRUDENCE. On horseback.

JESSICA. On horseback! What do you mean on horseback?

PRUDENCE. He's on a horse. Didn't we say that?

JESSICA. No, you didn't say that. Nobody said anything about a horse. I don't work with animals.

GILLIAN. I thought you did that act with the poodle?

JESSICA. That wasn't me!

POLLY. It's not a big horse. It's a little horse.

JESSICA. I don't care if it's a stunted Shetland pony, I'm not doing it.

PRUDENCE. Jessica, it's not a real horse. It's part of the figure.

POLLY. Think of it as a costume challenge, dear. *(Starting toward kitchen.)* I know, I'll get you a horse. You go ahead, I'll be right back.

(POLLY exits Kitchen.)

KENDALL. How long do I just stand here? I'm just standing here with everybody looking at me.
LACEY. Oh, well, let's see, it's ....
PRUDENCE. *(Fast.)* It's Ermintrude on, Gundra on, Gundra off, Knight on, Knight off, Gundra on, Gundra off with Ermintrude.
LACEY. See, it's not long.

(POLLY rushes in from the kitchen with a mop or squeegee mop.)

POLLY. Okay, Jessica, this will help you.

(Hands mop to JESSICA.)

JESSICA. What is this?
POLLY. It's a horse, a little hobby horse.
JESSICA. This little horse is wet.
POLLY. Yes, well I did the kitchen this morning.
LACEY. Okay, are we ready? It's the knight in shining armor ...
GILLIAN. Astride a squeegee.
LACEY. ... on horseback from Stage Left. And ....
JESSICA. *(Not moving.)* What's my motivation?
PRUDENCE. What do you mean?
JESSICA. Why am I here? Where did I come from? And why am I riding this damp little horse over there?
GILLIAN. Because that's how a clockwork clock works.
LACEY. So, ready, it's knight in shining armor from Left to Center.

(JESSICA does this—the horse is frisky—ending up directly behind, Upstage, of KENDALL.)

LACEY. As a director, I never thought I'd say this, but Jessica, could you make your performance a little more mechanical.

PRUDENCE. *(Looking at notes.)* I think she's in the wrong place. Yes. Jessica, you should be in front of Kendall.

JESSICA. Downstage!? With Kendall upstage!?

PRUDENCE. Yes, it's clockwork. All the figures are on their own tracks.

JESSICA. *(Moving directly in front of and blocking KENDALL.)* I should have tried out for Hedda Gabbler at the community theater.

KENDALL. *(Edging into view.)* I feel kinda silly.

GILLIAN. I don't know why, you're not the one standing there in German drag, holding a wet mop.

JESSICA. *(Throwing down mop.)* That's it! That is it!

POLLY. *(Reproving.)* Gillian! *(To JESSICA.)* Now, Jessica, dear, we need you to do this.

PRUDENCE. *(Under.)* Yes, we do.

(KENDALL puts arm around JESSICA.)

LACEY. *(Under.)* You were very good.

POLLY. ... We're one short already. It'll be fun. Really. You know how Gillian is. Pay no attention.

JESSICA. I'm telling Henry about you.

GILLIAN. Henry already knows about me.

POLLY. Now come on. Calm down.

JESSICA. Well, okay. What do I do now?

GILLIAN. Well, they always say you should get right back on the horse.

(KENDALL hands JESSICA "horse.")

LACEY. You ride off to the Stage Right archway.

JESSICA. *(Doing so.)* This isn't even a cameo; I'm an extra.

KENDALL. I'm still just standing here doing nothing.

PRUDENCE. *(To LACEY.)* You know, maybe we should add the movements now.

(LACEY nods.)

POLLY. Oh, good idea. *(To kitchen.)* I'll go and get some props to help. Be right back.

(POLLY exits to kitchen.)

JESSICA. Does everybody have movements?
PRUDENCE. Nearly everybody.
LACEY. Right, Saint Ermintrude, here we are. Kendall, you're gathering flowers.
KENDALL. Okay. *(Drops to her knees and starts gathering.)* Well, it's better than just standing there, I guess.
PRUDENCE. I don't think the figures are that flexible. It's more symbolic.
LACEY. You know, we may all be missing the symbolism here. These are archetypal figures: Death and a Maiden, an Angel, Vice and Virtue. We have a chance to make this relevant and resonant; the timeless conflict of good and ....
POLLY. *(Entering from the kitchen.)* Okay, I turned on the crab, and I got some stuff to help. *(She is carrying a wicker basket of plastic flowers, a dustpan, and a long-handled feather duster.)* It was the best I could do.
GILLIAN. Hurry up, Polly, you're just in time to stop symbolism.
POLLY. *(Putting dustpan and duster down, takes basket to KENDALL who rises.)* Here we are. She's gathering them into the basket.
KENDALL. *(Stage whisper.)* Mother, these are plastic.
POLLY. I know, dear, they always look fresh. And we won't need new ones next time. Pretty, aren't they?

PRUDENCE. She sort of takes a flower and holds it out to one side then brings it back to the basket. *(KENDALL starts doing this.)* And then the same thing with the other hand. And so on.

POLLY. We'll fix the basket to the costume, then it'll be easier. But isn't it fun?

JESSICA. Listen, does the knight come on again, or was that it?

PRUDENCE. Yes, the knight comes on again.

LACEY. But now it's Evil Pagan Queen Gundra, from ... er ... Stage Right.

GILLIAN. *(Moving to position.)* And what are my movements?

PRUDENCE. You're shaking.

GILLIAN. Shaking! Why am I shaking?

JESSICA. Old age.

POLLY. *(Handing her he dustpan.)* You're shaking your battle axe.

JESSICA. Oh, God is good. *(With her mop.)* Well, Gillian, welcome to the Glockenspiel Cleaning Ladies.

GILLIAN. *(To POLLY, meaning dustpan.)* This was the best you could do?

POLLY. I could've brought a cleaver, but I thought someone might get hurt.

GILLIAN. Someone still might.

LACEY. *(Slowly as GILLIAN does it.)* And Gundra comes on stage ... and to center stage ... downstage of Ermintrude.

KENDALL. Am I still gathering?

PRUDENCE. You're still gathering.

JESSICA. And the old battle-axe is still shaking.

PRUDENCE. They go off together.

(GILLIAN has turned around and she and KENDALL go off Left.)

LACEY. And Gundra summons Death.

POLLY. *(Grabbing the feather duster.)* Me, that's me.

KENDALL. What are you doing with the duster?

POLLY. I didn't have a scythe in the kitchen. Now where am I?

LACEY. You're over here. Stage Right. And you go on and round ... and off to Gundra's castle. Swinging your *(She stops because POLLY had done this, swinging the scythe enthusiastically.)* Great.

POLLY. I'm having more fun.

JESSICA. And now who's on?

PRUDENCE. The second Saint Ermintrude. It's Ermintrude in the sack *(On hearing this POLLY turns and rushes off Up Center to the rest of the house. Exits.)* about to be thrown into the river to drown.... And she's brought on by Death.

LACEY. Polly.

GILLIAN. Who's not here.

JESSICA. I could do it.

KENDALL. I hope this isn't too much for Mother. All this rushing around and excitement.

PRUDENCE. When are we doing this again? I like to be home when Nando's home.

LACEY. Sunday?

KENDALL. Mother goes to church.

JESSICA. We do too.

PRUDENCE. Monday?

JESSICA. Driving Henry to his therapist.

PRUDENCE. Monday evening?

KENDALL. Mother starts her aerobics class. I signed her up. Oh, and I forgot to tell her.

PRUDENCE. Tuesday?

KENDALL. Mother's at the library. I've got Tai Chi.

PRUDENCE. Tuesday evening?

LACEY. I'm teaching.

PRUDENCE. Wednesday.

JESSICA. Driving Henry to get his allergy shots.

PRUDENCE. Wednesday evening? Oh, no I've got a client coming. Thursday?

JESSICA. Driving Henry to his other therapist.

LACEY. *(Irked.)* Doesn't Henry drive?

JESSICA. Well, of course he drives. But he gets a little tense if he's going to the doctor or the therapists or the movies. Brilliant but high-strung. And don't misunderstand me: I adore Henry.

GILLIAN. And I adore Henry, too. Especially now he's married to Jessica.

PRUDENCE. Thursday evening?

GILLIAN. No.

KENDALL. *(Simultaneously.)* No. Thursday evening I have a Home Again, Home Again meeting here.

GILLIAN. Home Again. Home Again?

JESSICA. Ha, ha. *(GILLIAN and KENDALL look at JESSICA.)* For short. Home Again—Ha. Home Again, Home Again—Ha, Ha.

KENDALL. *(Sour.)* Very funny.

(Unnoticed by the others, POLLY enters Up Center from the rest of the house. She carries a very large, filled laundry bag. She also carries, though it may not be apparent, an accordion or concertina, which she sets down on the sofa.)

GILLIAN. Just what is this Home Again thing?

KENDALL. It's a support group for returning adult children. They need support.

GILLIAN. I thought they were getting support by being Home Again, Home Again. You certainly are.

JESSICA. Well, it can't be Thursday. It's the first Thursday in the month and that's when Polly and Gillian always get together. Red Thursday.

KENDALL. Why red?

GILLIAN. Because after we've made some martinis and kicked off our shoes, we throw big red steaks on a big red grill and open a big red bottle of wine.

KENDALL. *(Annoyed.)* That's disgusting. It's primitive, it's pagan ....

GILLIAN. *(Implacable)* And it's Thursday.

JESSICA. Listen, you two, why don't we let Polly decide.

POLLY. I've already decided; we should get on with this rehearsal. *(Hoisting laundry bag.)* I've got a Saint in a Sack.

LACEY. Okay, everybody, let's clear the stage. Now it's Death from the Right ...

KENDALL. But she ended up on the left.

PRUDENCE. The figures actually go all the way around in a circle.

LACEY. ... from the Right with Ermintrude in a sack. *(POLLY "enters" brandishing her duster/scythe. She uses the drawstring of the laundry bag to bounce the bag up and down.)* To Center. That's right. *(POLLY stops Center, but continues bouncing the laundry bag. Pause.)* Does anyone want to ask why?

GILLIAN. I think what's really frightening is that the answer is going to make sense.

JESSICA. Polly, why are you bouncing the Saint in a Sack?

POLLY. Well, this Ermintrude has movements, too. She keeps popping her head up out of the sack. I'm just giving a sense of that.

GILLIAN. Told you.

LACEY. And Death goes off left, leaving Ermintrude Center.

POLLY. *(As she goes.)* Still popping up and down.

LACEY. Still popping. And the knight rides on from the left.

JESSICA. And what's my movement?

LACEY. *(To PRUDENCE.)* What's her movement?

PRUDENCE. *(Looking at notes.)* Wait a minute. Doesn't have one.

LACEY. *(To JESSICA.)* You don't have one.

JESSICA. Whaddya' mean, I don't have one!? Even the pathetic sack has a movement. Well, mark my words, Jessica Sheridan is not going to be out-acted and upstaged by a wriggling, twitching, spastic laundry bag.

POLLY. She's not spastic; she's drowning.

JESSICA. She deserves to—scene-stealer.

GILLIAN. Jessica, it's not actually moving now.

LACEY. So it's Knight on from the Left *(JESSICA does this.)* ... and down and round ...

JESSICA. *(Stops at sack. To sack.)* You've met your match. You move; I move. So watch it.

(JESSICA continues round and off.)

LACEY. ... and off Right.

GILLIAN. Well, we may not have symbolism, but I think we've nailed theater-of-the absurd.

POLLY. You know, every time a figure comes on the clock bell strikes. Mary was going to bring her gong, and I don't have one. But maybe we should indicate it.

KENDALL. Tell me you don't want one of us standing around going boing?

LACEY. Well, maybe not boing.

GILLIAN. Ding-dong.

PRUDENCE. The knight doesn't come on again.

POLLY. And Jessica, dear, you wanted lines.

JESSICA. You're not serious. Who in their right mind would stand around going ding-dong?

GILLIAN. The same person who just spoke to a laundry bag.

LACEY. Who's on next?

PRUDENCE. *(Moving to position. POLLY gets accordion.)* It's my turn. Death and the Angel. Simultaneously.

POLLY. *(Handing PRUDENCE the accordion.)* Here you are, dear.

PRUDENCE. What's this?

POLLY. It's an accordion. I don't have a harp.

PRUDENCE. I'm glad you don't have a grand piano.

LACEY. Death on the Right, Angel on the Left. Ready. And the clock strikes.

JESSICA. *(Flat.)* Ding-dong.

LACEY. *(As POLLY and PRUDENCE move.)* And Death and the Angel meet at Center. And struggle over Ermintrude. *(POLLY and PRUDENCE somewhat at a loss.)* I think just a slightly back and forth. *(Which they do.)* Good, good, And the Angel wins. Death goes off empty-handed. *(Which POLLY does.)* And the Angel goes off.

(Which PRUDENCE does, taking the laundry bag.)

PRUDENCE. *(As she goes.)* I've got Ermintrude.

POLLY. *(As she goes.)* Be sure and bounce her.

KENDALL. You won't have to really carry the Saint, will you?

(During this, POLLY takes the hassock upstage to the mounted fish, positions hassock, climbs up on it, and takes down fish. Replaces hassock, goes back and gets fish.)

PRUDENCE. Oh, no, I hope not. She'll be in the sack, won't she?

LACEY. We can cut little holes for her feet in the bottom of the sack, and if the sack is big enough and droops down, no one will even see them.

LACEY. And now it's ... it's me, finally. Saint Ermintrude. And I'm from the Left.

PRUDENCE. And I've gone all the way around and come back on the Left, too.

JESSICA. Playing the harp.

(PRUDENCE squeezes the accordion.)

GILLIAN. The harp, not the accordion.

POLLY. *(Handing LACEY the plaque with the fish.)* And Racy Lacey this is for you.

LACEY. Gee thanks.

POLLY. Her basket of flowers has been miraculously transformed into a basket of fish, which she distributes to the poor. That's your movement. It's just like the flowers. Only it's fish.

LACEY. The things I do for tenure.

POLLY. We'll try and get you pretty fish.

PRUDENCE. *(Moving as does LACEY.)* And we come and we go to Center.

(Where PRUDENCE and LACEY stay.)

JESSICA. Ding-dong. Ding-dong.

LACEY. And now ... I don't have my notes.

PRUDENCE. Neither do I.

KENDALL. *(Who has picked up a set of notes.)* Death comes on to claim her victim.

JESSICA. Ding-dong.

KENDALL. Mother. *(POLLY enters right.)* All the way across. *(Which POLLY does.)* And claims the Evil Pagan Queen Gundra.

POLLY. Come on Gillian, we're the final scene.

KENDALL. *(As POLLY and GILLIAN do it.)* And brings her on, and take her round, and off. To her doom.

PRUDENCE. *(Starting off Left.)* And we go off Left, the way we came. *(Which they do.)* I've a feeling there's something wrong.

LACEY. Great. That's it. We've done it.

GILLIAN. Now that I'm doomed, can I please have a cigarette?

POLLY. There's one more thing, isn't there?

JESSICA. Well, I'd better be in it.

POLLY. Well, of course you are, dear. It's the Grande Finale. *(Enthusiastic.)* The bells ring out joyously and all the figures come on and go round.

LACEY. It's everybody, in order of appearance, from the right. Everybody get your props.

KENDALL. Someone get the sack.

(POLLY gets sack and has a thought.)

POLLY. Wait. Prudence, I've remembered what's wrong. When you and Lacey just went off, that was wrong. You can't go backwards.

LACEY. But we're supposed to go off Left.

POLLY. Yes, but we're all fixed on tracks in circles. We can't turn around; we're always facing the same way. I mean, we can go backwards, but we can't backwards forwards. Either we go forwards forward, or backwards backward. And the ones who're facing front are always facing front they're going left or going right, doing movements, facing front and moving sideways.

GILLIAN. And those extremely lucky people would be?

PRUDENCE. The three Saints.

GILLIAN. Thank God, I'm not a Saint.

KENDALL. Not even close.

JESSICA. How do you make a horse go backwards?

LACEY. Let's just do it.

(The order of crossing will be: KENDALL facing Front, Gillian facing Right, JESSICA facing Right, POLLY facing Left, PRUDENCE facing Right, LACEY facing Front. POLLY and PRUDENCE carry the sack between them.)

LACEY. Polly, why don't you start us off.

POLLY. Ladies, on three.

LACEY. *(Intense.)* And we need energy, commitment, truth; we don't want it to be a farce.

GILLIAN. Better farce than domestic drama.

POLLY. Wait. I know. *(Steps forward out of her place in line. Performs her cheer with energy and commitment. Funkier than we might have expected.)*
>One o'clock
>>Two o'clock
>>>Three o'clock chime
>Glockenspiel girls let's tell the time

> One o'clock
> Two o'clock
> Fast not slow
> Glockenspiel girls let's go, go, go!

(And they go. They curve from Right to Down Center, Up and off Left. All doing their movements with their props. In a line, close together. POLLY and PRUDENCE also as best they can bouncing the sack between them JESSICA does "ding-dongs.")

POLLY. *(As they go.)* Joyously, Jessica, joyously! *(They "exit" Left.)* And back again!

(Which they do, "exit" Right, and immediately disperse a little.)

KENDALL. Thank Heavens, that's over.

POLLY. *(Simultaneously.)* Wasn't that fun?

JESSICA. *(Simultaneously.)* I'm never ding-donging again.

LACEY. *(Clapping her hands for attention.)* Okay, ladies, from the top.

POLLY. No, wait! It's lunchtime.

JESSICA. Bless you, Polly.

GILLIAN. You're a saint.

POLLY. It's all very informal. *(Gestures to kitchen.)* In there. And who hasn't been here before? Prudence, Lacey, there's a bathroom there *(kitchen)* and there *(rest of house)* of course. Kendall, can you .... *(KENDALL crosses to kitchen door, LACEY and PRUDENCE following. Simultaneously GILLIAN goes to her bag for a cigarette. Simultaneously JESSICA goes to the drinks table.)* Be sure and try the crab dip.

KENDALL. Do you all know that crabs are scavengers? *(As LACEY and PRUDENCE pass her and exit.)* The food is booby-trapped with cream and butter.

(KENDALL exits behind LACEY and PRUDENCE.)

POLLY. *(Crossing to kitchen.)* Come on you two.

(POLLY exits.)

JESSICA. Be right there.

(GILLIAN, seated, has taken a cigarette and lighter out of her purse, but the lighter doesn't work.)

GILLIAN. I really am doomed.

JESSICA. *(Pouring a glass of water.)* How's that? *(GILLIAN demonstrates lighter doesn't work.)* Oh, sorry. Maybe Polly has one.

GILLIAN. She usually has ashtrays around.

JESSICA. *(Crossing in.)* It doesn't matter, you're not smoking. *(Sitting.)* I wish this were vodka.

GILLIAN. I wish this were lit.

JESSICA. You know, there's something about Polly I've been meaning to ask. Kendall sort of said she's worried about Polly; that she's flustered and dithery and rushed. I don't think that's true do you?

GILLIAN. Yes, I do.

JESSICA. You do? Since Bill died?

GILLIAN. No, not since Bill died.

(KENDALL opens kitchen door.)

KENDALL. Gillian, Jessica, Mother said come eat.

JESSICA. *(To kitchen.)* Okay, coming. *(To GILLIAN as she goes.)* I'll see if Polly has a lighter.

(JESSICA exits kitchen.)

KENDALL. She doesn't. Gillian?

GILLIAN. In a minute.

KENDALL. *(Letting kitchen door close behind her.)* Gillian, there's no smoking.

GILLIAN. Believe me, I'm not smoking.

KENDALL. It's for your own good, you know.

GILLIAN. *(Rising.)* Polly smokes.

KENDALL. Not anymore. I've been worried about her, so I'm helping change her lifestyle. She's feeling much better, and I'm not having you undermine that, Gillian. Bad people tempt and recruit so you won't be alone with your vices.

GILLIAN. And good people know what's best for everyone.

KENDALL. I know what's best for Mother. I'm going to make her healthy and productive and confident. I'm going to give her self-esteem.

GILLIAN. Well, you've got plenty to give.

KENDALL. You don't get it, do you? You rule your own selfish little world. The occasional lunch, the occasional dinner, the more than occasional drink and the incessant cigarettes. What kind of life is that? Just what, if anything, do you stand for?

GILLIAN. Live and let live. Remember that?

KENDALL. There ought to be laws about people like you.

GILLIAN. Well, you've got the smoking law.

KENDALL. That's just a start; there'll be other laws. Your reign here is over. I'm taking Mother out of your world. There'll be no more Red Thursdays. Ding-dong, Gillian, the Evil Pagan Queen is dead.

POLLY. *(Enters from kitchen. At kitchen door.)* What are you doing out here? *(Beat.)* Everybody's eating. It turned out very well, so I opened a bottle of wine, just to help it all go down. *(On hearing this, KENDALL swivels and storms to the kitchen. POLLY surprised, as KENDALL exits.)* Kendall, I didn't think you liked wine, dear. *(Crossing to GILLIAN.)* Aren't you hungry?

GILLIAN. Not really.

POLLY. Well, isn't the clock fun? Don't you think it's going well?

GILLIAN. *(Putting an arm around POLLY.)* Yes, Polly, "dear." *(Both smile.)* The clock is fully wound ... and ready to strike the hour.

(Curtain.)

END OF ACT I

ACT II

(In the darkness, we hear a large gong struck loudly. The furniture has all been pulled back from its ACT I position almost to the walls, leaving more of the room/stage clear. The folding screen is positioned Up Center as the "face" of the clock. Its Stage Left panel is angled back such that a character entering from the kitchen may not notice a character behind the screen. The hassock is down Left. The straight-backed chair and a kitchen stepstool are Center in front of the screen. This arrangement will force the action Front and Center, which is a good thing. There is a sewing basket there. Part of Gundra's costume hangs over the screen. Right of the screen is a gong—preferably large and free-standing in its own mounting, or if smaller, on the occasional table which has been moved to that position. There is a large Oriental rug/carpet Center.
KENDALL *is costumed as a medieval nun [habit not black] with a halo; she is studying a sheet of paper.* LACEY *in street clothes similar to those in ACT I, is seated Center sewing on her costume. There is a basket of yellow plastic daffodils beside her.* GILLIAN, *also seated, in street clothes is studying her lines.* JESSICA, *in slacks or jeans and a top, holding at her side a little triangular pennant is standing by the gong.* JESSICA *strikes the gong a second time. And a third.)*

GILLIAN. Jessica, if you do that again, your children are going to be motherless.

JESSICA. Well, I like it. Now that we have the gong, I don't have to stand around saying ding-dong, ding-dong. I hated saying ding-dong.

GILLIAN. Jessica, you are standing around saying ding-dong.

JESSICA. You are such a pill.

KENDALL. Well, I'm certainly glad Lacey and I switched our parts before Mary gave us our lines to learn.

GILLIAN. Why did you switch parts?

LACEY. Costumes.

JESSICA. I still have to learn my lines.

KENDALL. Well, you've got a small part.

JESSICA. There are no small parts just small writers. But *(Holding it up.)* there are small pennants; look at this—it's pathetic. You can't make and entrance waving this. *(Heading Up Stage.)* I'm going to fix this wretched pennant to my lance. And I'm going to learn my lines. Both of them.

(JESSICA exits to rest of house.)

KENDALL. Originally, I didn't think we were going to have any lines.

LACEY. *(Grim.)* Yes. I'm very sorry to say Mary rhymed her translation of the story, and assigned us parts.

> Once there was a heathen altar where the clock-tower stands
>
> Cruel as thunder evil Gundra ruled those pagan lands.

GILLIAN. *(Under.)* That's me.

LACEY.

> It was a time of darkness, of deeds and manners crude
>
> But free of vice and very nice was saintly Ermintrude

GILLIAN. *(Appalled.)* Oh, dear. Well now we know what was wrong with Mary last week. She obviously came down with a severe case of galloping doggerel.

KENDALL. Is this going to work?

GILLIAN. Just go with the fact that it's doggerel. Say it loud and clear, keep the rhythm and hit the rhymes.

(GILLIAN rises.)

LACEY. This better look good on my resume. *(As GILLIAN starts to kitchen.)* Where are you going?
GILLIAN. *(Turns in.)* I'm looking for my helmet. Seen it?

(The phone rings.)

LACEY. *(Focus phone. Simultaneously to GILLIAN.)* No, sorry.
KENDALL. *(Simultaneously.)* I'll get it. *(Facing in from near the kitchen door, GILLIAN sees something behind the screen, crosses in and goes behind the screen. Simultaneously KENDALL goes Right to the phone. Into phone.)* Hello.... Yes.... No, this is Kendall, her daughter.... Oh, hello, Mrs. Wilson.... Betty.... Er, no she's not right now.... Thank you, yes we love it.... Yes, quite large.... Five.... Four and a half.... Oh, no, no it's not for sale.... Yes it would, but there won't be just one person, I'm staying here too.... Well, thank you, but she won't be changing her mind. Bye. *(Hangs up. To LACEY.)* Word is out there's a widow with a large house.
LACEY. She could get a lot for it.
KENDALL. Oh, no. I have plans for it.
LACEY. Renting rooms? I may have to get a roommate myself.
KENDALL. No, I have another idea. Now where's Prudence? She's late and we can't start without her.
LACEY. Well, if I had Nando at home I'd be late too. Now there's a knight in shining armor.
KENDALL. How's that going?
LACEY. This Thursday after class; it's inevitable I can tell. He's hot for it.

(During this the hanging costume is slowly pulled off the folding

screen from behind.)

KENDALL. You know, Prudence is going to be just like them. They just live their lives. It's not that they're bad—they're not really that bad, they're just not good. They don't even know what's good for them. Gillian's the worst of them; she has the social conscience of a Troglodyte. But Mother could be good; she just needs a little push.

LACEY. Is Mary like them, too?

KENDALL. Mary! Where's Mary? We can't start without her, either.

POLLY. *(Entering from the kitchen with a basket of yellow fish. Fussing with fish she does not see GILLIAN. She also carries a grotesquely ugly rubber Halloween mask.)* Kendall, dear, I've got your fish. They're very pretty. We just need to make sure they match Lacey's flowers. Oh, they do. Good, good. *(KENDALL takes basket.)* I want it all to look pretty on television. *(Hands LACEY the daffodils.)* These are yours, Lacey.

LACEY. Thank you.

POLLY. Kendall, I think you're the only one ready; I'm proud of you, dear. As soon as Prudence and Mary get here, we can start.

LACEY. Then I'd better get ready, too. I'm going to change. *(Indicating rest of house.)* May I?

POLLY. Of course, you can. There's lots of room.

LACEY. I'll return as a virtuous maiden.

POLLY. We won't recognize you, dear.

LACEY. Even I won't recognize me.

(LACEY exits UC to rest of house without a backward glance; does not see GILLIAN.)

KENDALL. Mother, are you sure you're up for all this?

POLLY. Of course, I am. I'm glad there's plenty of room for everybody to change.

KENDALL. There's so much room, we should be using it to help people. And get some income.

POLLY. You mean rent rooms, take in borders?

KENDALL. Well, that's a little old-fashioned. You actually sort of give them the rooms for free because you care about them, then you form a non-profit organization and apply for grants and subsidies and solicit deductible donations and the government pays too.

POLLY. Is that legal?

KENDALL. Completely. And profitable.

POLLY. Well, you know Gillian and I have talked about me moving into her guest house. It's a lovely guest house, small but everything built-in and right beside the pool.

KENDALL. And what about this?

POLLY. Well, I'd sell it?

KENDALL. And what about me?

POLLY. Well. Well, I don't think they're hiring at the library, dear.

KENDALL. Mother, we could use the house to help people.

POLLY. What sort of people?

KENDALL. People who need help. I'm the kind of person who cares about people who need help. And since I'll be here, I can help you too.

POLLY. Oh, thank you? *(Beat.)* Do I need help? I didn't know I needed help.

KENDALL. Well, we all need help sometimes. It's just since Father died you've been a little, well, flustered, absent-minded.

POLLY. Have I, dear? Sorry. I do wish everybody would get here. Where's Gillian?

GILLIAN. *(Loudly from behind SL end of screen.)* I'm right here, Polly. (POLLY and KENDALL are both startled. Both focus SL end of screen. GILLIAN comes from behind SR end of screen, fully costumed as Evil Pagan Queen Gundra. Essentially a full, classic Brunhilde outfit: long yellow braids, winged or horned helmet, breastplate,*

shield, but an axe instead of a spear.) Fully-armed. Ready to do battle
with the good and the virtuous.

POLLY. Gillian, I've got something to ask you: Do I need help?

GILLIAN. *(Quoting KENDALL.)* Well, we all need help sometimes. The question is with what? Right now, I need help in back.
(Turning her back to POLLY.) Would you?

POLLY. *(Fastening something on GILLIAN's costume.)* Certainly, dear. There you are. Where is everybody else?

KENDALL. Well, Lacey and Jessica are changing. And Mary
and Prudence aren't here yet.

POLLY. Oh, dear. Kendall, can you go and see how they're doing and if they need help.

KENDALL. Sure. You'd better get changed yourself, Mother.
(Looking GILLIAN up and down.) You know something, Gillian, that
suits you perfectly.

(KENDALL exits UC to rest of house.)

POLLY. I don't think she likes you.

GILLIAN. I know she doesn't like me.

POLLY. Thinks you're a bad influence. Do you mind?

GILLIAN. I'm used to it. I've spent most of my life coming under criticism from the Moral Right, but lately I'm getting pressured by
the Virtuous Left, and let me tell you something Polly, they're equally
annoying. A plague on both their houses.

POLLY. Speaking of houses, Kendall thinks we can make some
money from this one.

GILLIAN. Rent rooms?

POLLY. Apparently that's old-fashioned.

GILLIAN. I thought you wanted to move into my place?

POLLY. Well, I do, or I did. But then Kendall came home again.
Now I don't know. I just don't know, Gillian, if I did come to your
place, I don't want to learn to speak Swahili.

GILLIAN. Polly, I don't know Swahili. I can't even spell Swahili.

POLLY. What I mean is I don't want to be pushed·into pottery classes, or learn to dance the tango, or take up rock climbing. I don't want to be new and improved.

GILLIAN What do you want to do?

POLLY. Well, I think I want to do a little gardening and sit by the pool and read cookbooks.

GILLIAN. Then that's what you'll do.

POLLY. Oh, good. Is that a bad thing to want?

GILLIAN. Terrible. You should be ashamed of yourself. We're supposed to be energetic and engaged and contributing. On the go all the time like Jessica. And healthy, healthy, healthy. Healthiness is the new morality. But, Polly, I'll tell you a secret.

POLLY. I thought you knew everything, dear.

GILLIAN. Not this. It's not pretty. I made a fortune with no ambition at all, because, and this is the ugly part, what I really wanted to do was spend my life devouring cheap novels and expensive chocolates. *(Beat.)* But then came mathematics and writing code and Henry and you know all that.

POLLY. Well, you can do it now, dear.

GILLIAN. I've outgrown my taste for cheap novels.

POLLY. And chocolates?

GILLIAN. Now you're talking.

POLLY. Bill and Kendall loved this house. She's smart like Bill. She was always Daddy's girl, you know. And I just wonder if maybe I should stay here and help her help people. She loves helping people.

GILLIAN. Yes. Is she a lot of help around the house?

POLLY. Well, er ... not, she doesn't really vacuum, but she does help.

GILLIAN. How?

POLLY. Well, er.... *(Pleased.)* She did lunch today! And I'm starving; I haven't eaten.

GILLIAN. What are we having?

POLLY. Crudités. With a nice yogurt-tofu dip.

GILLIAN. Polly, are you telling me that I got all dressed up as an Evil Pagan Queen for raw cauliflower?

POLLY. And broccoli, and ... I'm sorry, dear. But it's organic cauliflower and broccoli. Very expensive. We have to drive all over town in her great big SUV to find it. But we're saving a lot of money on electricity, because most of the stuff doesn't get cooked.

GILLIAN. I thought that was Dylan's SUV?

POLLY. Well, it was till they got divorced.

GILLIAN. Dylan was a nice guy. Why exactly did they get divorced?

POLLY. He was cheating on her.

GILLIAN. I don't believe it!

POLLY. It's true. She caught him cheating—she caught him at McDonald's, Burger King, and even over here.

GILLIAN. Polly, you helped break up her marriage.

POLLY. It was just barbequed ribs, for Heaven's sakes. I felt sorry for poor Dylan. Now I feel guilty. And I'd like grandchildren.

GILLIAN. Well, she'll probably get married again. More men have to suffer.

POLLY. You never wanted to get married again, did you?

GILLIAN. Lord, no. I had enough trouble off-loading Henry onto poor Jessica.

POLLY. She still thinks she seduced him away from you.

GILLIAN. I know she does.

(The doorbell rings.)

POLLY. *(Calls.)* It's open. *(To GILLIAN.)* Well, if it's Mary, she just has to get in the sack; I've cut little holes for the feet.

(PRUDENCE enters. She is dressed as an angel with a halo, but

carries her very large wings as well as her harp. She is wet and disheveled.)

PRUDENCE. Sorry I'm late; it's starting to rain and I got pulled over. *(Coming in to playing area.)* Did you know that in this county it's illegal for a pregnant angel to drive down the street with her left wing hanging out of the driver's side window?

GILLIAN. I thought everyone knew that.

POLLY. I am sorry. Did you get a ticket?

PRUDENCE. Just a stern warning.

POLLY. Oh, good. Now as soon as Mary gets here, we can start.

PRUDENCE. Mary isn't coming, didn't she tell you?

GILLIAN. *(Grim.)* No, she didn't.

PRUDENCE. *(Crossing DL to sit on the hassock. To work with her wings will set the harp leaning against the downstage side of the hassock.)* I think when she heard about the TV station coming she had second thoughts. She's ordered a stunning designer gown and a spotlight and she's going to introduce us and do the commentary.

GILLIAN. Don't tell Jessica about the spotlight; she'll want one.

POLLY. Oh, but who's going to be in the sack? What do we do?

PRUDENCE. She said she's sure we'll find someone, and in the meantime muddle through. And she apologized in advance for using the word "ain't" but she had to.

POLLY. Oh, what'll we do? Gillian, what do we do now?

GILLIAN. Well, since that means we're all here, Polly, go and get changed.

POLLY. All right. *(Crossing up stage.)* At least, I won't have to get into character; I feel like death already.

(POLLY exits to rest of house, taking mask.)

PRUDENCE. Where is everybody? You said they're here.

GILLIAN. Lacey's changing. Jessica doing something with her

pennant. Polly's ... *(Gesture.)* And I don't know what Goody Two-Shoes is doing.

PRUDENCE. I don't know why I got changed at home. I think I thought it would be simpler. Is my halo on straight?

GILLIAN. Nearly.

(GILLIAN and PRUDENCE fix it.)

PRUDENCE. It's funny, I'm a tax accountant and Nando's in public relations and yet here we are both acting. He loves it. He stays after class. Maybe he really does want to be an actor.

GILLIAN. Do you think that's wise with a baby on the way?

PRUDENCE. No, no I don't. Ant I'd see even less of him. I don't see enough of him now since he started this class. We used to spend a lot of time together, well, all our time together, really.

GILLIAN. It's too big a gamble.

PRUDENCE. *(Thoughtful.)* Yes, yes it is, isn't it. *(Lightening.)* Jessica says you gamble. Big time.

GILLIAN. She would say that, but she's wrong. I went once to a casino with Henry. And that's where Henry and Jessica first saw each other. She was a dancer in the show. We ran into her afterwards and they were fascinated with each other. It was as if I wasn't there. But I saw my opportunity and I took it.

PRUDENCE. What did you do?

GILLIAN. Insisted, absolutely insisted that we go back to that casino over and over again. And it worked. I am now very good at black jack.

PRUDENCE. Why? You weren't in love with Henry?

GILLIAN. We were a pair of geeks, partners, fond of each other, made millions together, but not really in love. And Henry wanted children and I didn't. I'm not sure why he wanted children: they make him nervous. And he's not good with them. But Jessica is. Very good. She's even, God bless her, good with Henry.

PRUDENCE. You like her don't you?

GILLIAN. Well, of course, I like her. I wouldn't stick Henry with someone I didn't like.

PRUDENCE. Then why do you pick on her?

GILLIAN. Habit mostly. And it supports her idea that she's a femme fatale who seduced Henry away from me.

PRUDENCE. So you got divorced and they got married and you did all that for Henry?

GILLIAN. Well, not just for Henry. I mean, somebody had to get Jessica out of show business.

PRUDENCE. You know, I sort of wish Nando hadn't taken that acting class.

(LACEY enters from UC. She is in a traditional folk costume as a maiden [dirndl] very low-cut. Wherever her flowers, they do not obstruct the traffic-stopping cleavage. Comes Center.)

LACEY. Well, here I am a virtuous maiden. *(Twirls and poses.)* Convinced?

PRUDENCE. I definitely wish Nando hadn't taken that acting class. *(Smiles at LACEY.)* I was just saying Nando loves your class.

LACEY. Oh, thank you. He should, he's very good. Polly says Mary isn't coming, so maybe Nando could play the knight and Jessica could go in the sack.

GILLIAN. I dare you to tell Jessica that.

PRUDENCE. I don't think he'd have time anyway.

LACEY. Well, here we are an angel, a virgin, and a pagan queen. I can't believe I'm not the pagan queen.

GILLIAN. Neither can I.

PRUDENCE. *(Simultaneously.)* I can't either. *(ALL smile.)* Have you seen a stapler anywhere?

LACEY. No, sorry.

GILLIAN. I think there's one through there *(kitchen)* in the den.

Polly put out some stuff, glue, scissors, string, stuff.
PRUDENCE. *(Rising.)* Good. I had these things on once but the
police made me take them off. *(Crosses to kitchen, leaving her harp
onstage.)* I mean, I could just flap them with my arms, but then I
wouldn't be able to pluck my harp.

(PRUDENCE exits kitchen.)

GILLIAN. Are they nearly ready?
LACEY. Yes, I think so. Polly's having trouble with her death
mask. She says it's hot and makes her dizzy. Kendall's worried about
her. She say she's been shaky since her husband died.
GILLIAN. No, she hasn't. When Bill died she went through a
normal period of grief. But she wasn't shaky.
LACEY. And Prudence looked a bit under the weather.
GILLIAN. She was under the weather—it's raining, she's preg-
nant and she got stopped by the police.
LACEY. *(Indifferent.)* Poor little angel.
GILLIAN. You know, sometime even pagan queens are on the
side of the angels.
LACEY. What do you mean?
GILLIAN. I don't think she's on to you yet. But I am.
LACEY. What are you talking about?
GILLIAN. Evening classes
LACEY. Oh, well, that's none of your business, is it?
GILLIAN. I'm going to make it my business.
LACEY. Really. How are you going to do that?
GILLIAN. I'm going to make sure Nando fails his acting class.
LACEY. Are you kidding, he's terrific. Of the guys, he's the
best. I don't give many A plusses, but the physicality alone ....
GILLIAN. He's going to fail.
LACEY. How do you figure that?
GILLIAN. Because I'm not only very wealthy, I'm a pillar of this

community. I'm the one who arranged for the television station, the mayor, the sheriff and the dean of your college to come to our little pageant.

LACEY. *(Wary.)* Yes? So?

GILLIAN. So to you, your tenure at the college is a matter of work, research, publication, academic politics—very demanding. *(Deliberately.)* To me, your tenure is a phone call.

(Pause.)

LACEY. You wouldn't dare! You can't do this.

GILLIAN. Yes, I can. I just did. And by the way, Nando won't be staying after class.

LACEY. You can't control my private life! You've no right!

GILLIAN. Right? You are invoking right? You and Kendall think using the word cripple is a wrong, but breaking up a family is a right. Well, back off. *(Adamant.)* He won't be staying after class.

LACEY. You ... you really are an evil queen. Protecting poor little Prudence. Are you being good?

GILLIAN. Lord, I hope not, that always causes trouble.

LACEY. You think you can fix everything, don't you?

GILLIAN. No, I wish I could, but there's a problem here that's not mine to fix.

(POLLY and KENDALL, Death and the Saint, enter from UC. POLLY wears an enveloping, hooded black robe. She is wearing a plain translucent white mask, smooth, blank and featureless. [Not the one she was carrying before.] She carries a scythe which she will put aside till needed. Everyone who comes on stage is now in costume.)

POLLY. Well, here we are Death and the Saint. I had one of those rubber Halloween masks, but it was just too hot. So I used this.

Will I frighten the children?
GILLIAN. *(Dry.)* Well, not your children.
KENDALL. *(During the above, to LACEY.)* How's it going?
LACEY. *(Low.)* Fine.
KENDALL. What's the matter?
LACEY. *(Low.)* Nothing.
POLLY. I'm a little worried that I might forget my lines.

(PRUDENCE enters from the kitchen. She has her wings more or less on, and carries a paper or plastic plate with some food on it.)

PRUDENCE. Polly, I got something to eat.
POLLY. Oh, good for you, dear.
KENDALL. It really is good for you: no salt, no sugar, no fat, no preservatives... .
PRUDENCE. No, I raided the refrigerator, is that all right?
POLLY. Well, of course it is. Did you find something?
PRUDENCE. Yes, salami, a pickle and Hostess Twinkies.
KENDALL. Twinkies! *(Speaking to PRUDENCE, looking at POLLY.)* Where did you find Twinkies?
POLLY. *(Apologetic.)* Hidden under the bok choy, dear.
KENDALL. Mother! She's pregnant.
GILLIAN. How sharper than a serpent's tooth to have a junk food mother.
KENDALL. You stay out of this. *(Taking plate.)* Let me see that. What is this?
PRUDENCE. It's a snack.
KENDALL. Snack! It's a nutritional abyss.
GILLIAN. *(Taking plate.)* Give it back.
KENDALL. *(Not letting go.)* She can't eat this.
GILLIAN. *(Pulling.)* Of course, she can.
KENDALL. *(Tugging.)* No she can't. *(The plate tips and some food falls to the floor. KENDALL instantly lets go of the plate.)* Now

look what you've done.

LACEY. *(Juvenile.)* Food fight! Food fight!

POLLY. *(Takes plate, kneels, cleans up.)* Well, never mind.

GILLIAN. *(Overlapping.)* Polly, I'm sorry. I'll get it.

POLLY. No, no, it's all right. I've got it.

KENDALL. It's all over the carpet.

POLLY. It's all right. It's all right.

KENDALL. It's not all right. It just came back from the cleaners. It probably had to go to the cleaners because you spilled drinks and cigarette ash all over it.

POLLY. I wish it were cigarette ash; they say that keeps the moths out.

KENDALL. Now it's going to have to go back to the cleaners. And who's going to pay for that, you clumsy woman?

POLLY. Kendall, it's all right.

KENDALL. Mother, it is not all right.

POLLY. *(Rising.)* Yes, it is all right. *(Firmly.)* It wasn't at the cleaners, dear.

KENDALL. You said it was ....

POLLY. I know what I said but I wasn't telling the truth. I sold it because we needed the money. And Gillian saw it in the consignment shop and bought it and gave it back.

(POLLY moves Left to set down plate somewhere and ends up, as the others continue, unobtrusively taking it behind the screen.)

PRUDENCE. Oh, how nice.

LACEY. *(Sneers.)* Fixing things again.

KENDALL. Oh, yes, she thinks she can fix everything with her connections and her money. Everything but her own unenlightened life.

GILLIAN. I was trying to help because only one of the two people here is working and it's not you, you sanctimonious wretch.

KENDALL. Some of us, Gillian, are trying to make a better world. Some of us are trying to do good. But there you stand blocking the way, a Neanderthal impediment. Give up, Gillian, you're bound to lose. The deep-fried days are over. Things have changed and your chain-smoking, booze-swilling, self-indulgent, inconsiderate time has passed. *(Reasonable.)* Raise your consciousness. Don't be part of the problem, Gillian, be part of the solution. Make a virtue of necessity.

GILLIAN. *(Lethal.)* Your virtue has forced your own mother to hide food in her own home.

KENDALL. Don't you dare mention my mother! You corruption. You've undermined her health, her life-style and her stability. You know very well she's been stressed since my father died.

GILLIAN. No, she hasn't! If Polly's stressed, it's not since Bill died, it's since you came Home Again, Home Again, you sniveling little neo-Puritan virtucrat.

(There are three quick shattering strikes on the gong, forcing silence. Struck by POLLY, who has come to it from behind SR of screen.)

POLLY. Stop. Please stop. Just stop.

(The tension of the preceding breaks. LACEY, KENDALL, GILLIAN, and PRUDENCE look abashed.)

GILLIAN. *(Mutters.)* Sorry.

POLLY. Girls, girls, this isn't why people are coming to the Chamber of Commerce. I'm sure the Chamber of Commerce has quite enough on its hands without adding our squabbles. This isn't what people want to see. They want to see us in colorful, silly costumes running around because they hope to see us bump into each other. And our job is to rehearse so we don't bump into each other. So let's do that.

LACEY. *(Picking up stool and going Stage Left.)* Okay, let's clear for action.

(LACEY sets down stool out of playing area.)

GILLIAN. *(Moving chair and sewing basket Right.)* I've got the chair.

(With the furniture moved back and the rain outside, the now dark living room essentially disappears. There is the clear, very brightly lit, open playing area, with the folding screen as backdrop, and six characters in purely theatrical costumes.)

POLLY. Where's Jessica?
GILLIAN. Don't worry, she's never missed an entrance yet.
POLLY. Wait a minute, Who's going in the sack? I can't do it, I'm on at the same time. So's Jessica. And Prudence is pregnant.
KENDALL. *(Savoring it.)* Well, let's see, that leaves ....
LACEY. Gillian!
KENDALL. Gillian.
GILLIAN. I may not have time to get in the sack.
KENDALL. Don't worry, I'll shove you in.
LACEY. I'd be happy to help.
GILLIAN. Ah, the revenge of the little people.
POLLY. Then maybe I should strike the gong.
PRUDENCE. Oh, please let's do it once without the gong.
POLLY. Oh, all right, dear. Well, ready.
PRUDENCE. We're all set. If my wings stay on, we're all set.
LACEY. Take your places.

(Which means that they all go behind the screen, taking any necessary props, except for the harp which is forgotten. The stage is empty.)

GILLIAN. *(From behind the screen.)* Do you mind!

LACEY. *(From behind the screen.)* Excuse me.

POLLY. *(From behind the screen.)* On three. One, two, three.

KENDALL. *(Facing front, moving sideways distributing fish trundles on from Left of screen. All the ladies are now proficient in their mechanical movements.)*
"So evil is defeated and the world's a better place
And as for me ....

GILLIAN. *(From behind the screen, overlapping.)* Stop her.

LACEY. *(From behind the screen.)* Give me that scythe. *(LACEY enters not in "character" with the scythe, which she will use as a version of the hook to pull KENDALL off-stage. Hissing stage whisper.)* We changed parts, remember?

KENDALL. *(As she is pulled behind screen. Stage whisper.)* Sorry. I forgot, sorry.

POLLY. *(From behind the screen.)* Why did they change parts?

PRUDENCE. *(From behind the screen.)* Costumes.

GILLIAN. *(From behind the screen.)* Cleavage!

LACEY. *(Facing front, moving sideways, picking flowers enters Stage Right of screen. When she is Center, seductively.)*
"My name is Ermintrude and I'm a saint-in-waiting
I please the eye but please pass by I am not for dating
Here you see me coming with forest flowers laden
Free of vice and very nice, I am a Christian maiden

GILLIAN. *(Putting her face, and only her face around Stage Left of screen.)* You're supposed to be a Christian maiden gathering flowers, not a hooker turning tricks.

(GILLIAN withdraws. From far off we hear the sound of a horse approaching at a gallop.)

LACEY. Well, excuse me, I was trying to avoid the obvious interpretation.

PRUDENCE. *(Face only from Stage Left of screen.)* You go right ahead and be obvious, Lacey.

KENDALL. *(From behind the screen.)* What is that noise?

LACEY. *(Modified reading, sulky.)*

"Here you see me coming with forest flowers laden
Free of vice and very nice, I am a Christian maiden

GILLIAN. *(Facing the way she is going with axe chopping movements enters from Stage Left of screen. At Center.)*

"She only thinks of virtue and the Heavens that await her
Free of vice and very nice, ye gods, how much I hate her
(The hoof beats are now loud, and there are trumpets. Annoyed, GILLIAN repeats her last line very loudly.)

Free of vice and very nice, ye gods, how much I hate her

(GILLIAN exits Stage Right of screen. JESSICA enters [actually from the rest of the house UC] but she sweeps in fast to enter the playing area from behind the Stage Left screen. Hoof beats and fanfare. She is costumed as a knight on horseback [see production notes]. She carries a tiny audio player, putative source of the hoof beats. She also carries her lance, attached to which is not a pennant but a banner or flag of immense, stage dominating dimensions. Of a fabric that wafts and billows if flourished. And with JESSICA there are plenty of flourishes. She comes Center, completely blocking LACEY, reining in an obviously spirited horse. She jabs at a button on her player to stop the sound. The hoof beats continue. She jabs again. The hoof beats continue. To free up both hands she drapes the banner behind her over LACEY to support the lance. Using both hands tries to shut off the player. During this, the faces only of POLLY, Stage Right, and PRUDENCE and KENDALL, Stage Left one above the other.)

PRUDENCE. Oh, how clever.

(PRUDENCE withdraws.)

> KENDALL. *(Overlapping.)* She's mad, she's raving mad.
> POLLY. *(Overlapping.)* Isn't this fun?

(POLLY withdraws. GILLIAN enters from Stage Right of screen. Strides up to JESSICA, snatches the player out of her hands, hurls it to the floor and stomps it to death. At the third stomp, the sound ends.)

> KENDALL. *(Face only.)* And there was peace in the valley.

(KENDALL withdraws. GILLIAN has picked up the player and tossed it over the screen, whence we hear PRUDENCE scream, "Aahouch!")

> JESSICA. *(Beat.)* You hate me for my trumpets, don't you?
> GILLIAN. You and the horse you rode in on.

(GILLIAN exits Right of screen.)

> JESSICA. *(As GILLIAN goes, patting the horse's neck.)* Whoa, boy, whoa. Don't be frightened of the nasty lady.
>> "Here I am a gallant knight with chivalry imbued
>> Upon my steed with every deed I honor Ermintrude
>> Do not try, you Heathen Hordes, to harm or to alarm her
>> For who will fight to set it right the knight in shining armor
> *(Flat out addressing the audience which she can imagine, and not overly concerned with which way she's supposed to be facing.)* And then I'm supposed to go off with hoof beats and trumpets. But thanks to Gillian you're all just going to have to imagine the hoof beats and trumpets, while I trudge off in utter silence. *(Dejected, head hung, lance drooping, banner trailing JESSICA heads for Stage Right of*

screen.) It's no exit at all, really. No one will even notice me.

(JESSICA exits.)

GILLIAN. *(Entering Stage Left of screen, to Center.)*
"Faith, Hope, and Charity and thoughts of virtue fill her
Free of vice and very nice, I think I'll have to kill her

(GILLIAN turns and starts to led LACEY off Stage Left.)

LACEY. *(Stage whisper.)* Backwards, Gillian, backwards. Remember you can only face one way.
PRUDENCE. *(From behind the screen.)* I've lost my harp.
GILLIAN. *(Moving back to Center.)* Oh, all right.
"Free of vice and very nice, I think I'll have to kill her

(GILLIAN and LACEY move off Stage Left, mechanically doing their movements, exit.)

KENDALL. *(Face only, Stage Left of screen.)* Mother, where are you?
POLLY. *(From behind the screen.)* I'm waiting my cue, dear.
KENDALL. *(Face only, Stage Left of screen.)* Death doesn't have a cue; Death just comes on. *(Withdraws. From behind screen.)* Push her!
POLLY. *(Erupts, apparently pushed, from behind Stage Right screen, masked in the bland white mask with her scythe. At Center.)*
"When you're lost and lonely and you think you've gone astray
Stay with me and you will see Death always knows the way.
(POLLY exits Stage Left of screen. From behind the screen.) Hurry up, Gillian, we have to go right back out.
JESSICA. *(From behind the screen, shrieks.)* Hey! What are you doing?
PRUDENCE. *(From behind the screen.)* I'm looking for my harp.

JESSICA. *(From behind the screen.)* Well, it's not under there.
KENDALL. *(From behind the screen.)* Let me help.
GILLIAN. *(From behind the screen.)* Ouch!

(POLLY and GILLIAN enter Stage Right of screen. GILLIAN is in the sack, moving sideways, bobbing her head in and out of the sack. [see production note] She is not wearing her helmet, just the blonde wig with the yellow braids.)

POLLY.
"Now we come at last to the raging river's brink
This is Death so hold your breath, will she swim or sink?
For the maid the people prayed, but despite their wishes
Free of vice and very nice she now sleeps with the fishes.

(POLLY exits Stage Left of screen. Simultaneously, from Stage Right PRUDENCE, wings and halo perhaps awry, starts crawling out on her hands and knees, desperately trying to minimize her presence.)

GILLIAN.
"They always used to preach virtue is its own reward
(Becomes aware of PRUDENCE. Her delivery slows.)
So just why ... am I back as a saint in a sack, ... dear, Lord?
(PRUDENCE makes "pretend I'm not here" gestures.)
Free of vice and very nice, ah, but here's the rub
I am very scared my next line ... *(Dwindles watching PRU-DENCE.)* is glub, glub, glub.
PRUDENCE. *(Stage whisper.)* Don't let me interrupt you.
GILLIAN. Too late.
PRUDENCE. *(Stage whisper.)* I'm looking for my harp.
LACEY. *(Face only.)* What's going on out there?
GILLIAN. I'll tell you what's going on out here. There's a

winged, pregnant angel crawling around on all fours under the demented impression that it is somehow not an interruption.

(PRUDENCE has been attempting to crawl off unobtrusively with the harp, which is not easy.)

LACEY. *(Face only.)* Well, as long as we know.

(LACEY withdraws.)

GILLIAN. *(To PRUDENCE.)* I'm supposed to drown not die of old age.

PRUDENCE. *(Stage whisper.)* Do you think I should walk?

GILLIAN. You've got wings. Flutter off!

PRUDENCE. *(Jumps up and dashes off to Right end of screen. From behind the screen.)* Found it!

GILLIAN.
  "Free of vice and very nice, ah, but here's the rub
  I am very scared my next line is glub, glub, glub.
(Pause. Nothing happens. Loudly.)
  GLUB, GLUB, GLUB.
(Beat.) Will somebody who can walk erect get on out here.

JESSICA. *(Stage Left, face only, and possibly the horse's face only.)* I've lost my concentration. Can we start over?

GILLIAN. Start over! Are you mad? I'm not doing this twice.

JESSICA. *(Face only.)* Okay, where are we?

GILLIAN. *(Not happy.)* I don't know about you but I'm drowning in the Ninth Circle of Hell. Glub. Glub Glub!

JESSICA. *(Sallies forth.)*
  "Round and round in circles how long can it last
  Just keeping time I feel that I'm getting nowhere fast
  Round and round in circles until I want to drop
  All right sit tight this night this knight just might outright stop.

(To audience.) Remember the trumpets you had to imagine last time?
Well, imagine them again.

(JESSICA exits.)

>   KENDALL. *(From behind the screen.)* Mother!

(POLLY is pushed as before from Right of screen. Simultaneously,
PRUDENCE enters from Left of screen. PRUDENCE does not
have wings.)

>   POLLY. You found the harp.
>   PRUDENCE. *(Simultaneously.)* I found my harp.
>   GILLIAN. Pluck your harp!
>   POLLY. Where are your wings, dear?
>   PRUDENCE. *(Startled.)* Oh, my wings, I'll ....

(PRUDENCE turns to leave.)

>   GILLIAN. Pluck your wings, too!

(PRUDENCE turns back, minimizing, mouths "I think I'll just ...."
POLLY nods.)

>   PRUDENCE.
>   "Through the hosts of Heaven would welcome and affirm her
>   People's needs are goodly deeds right here on terra firma
>   POLLY.
>   "Now from whence to whither, with or without dismay
>   Stay with me and you will see Death always knows the way
>   PRUDENCE.
>   "Free of vice and very nice and finally sanctified
>   This dreadful fate you must abate and Death must stand aside

LACEY. *(Face only, Right of screen.)* Now tug of war.

(There is a mechanical, stylized tug of war. All three lean to the left simultaneously, then to the right, etc. During this:)

GILLIAN. *(Hisses.)* Take it easy.
KENDALL. *(From behind the screen.)* Pull her head off.
JESSICA. *(From behind the screen.)* This would be a good place for trumpets.
PRUDENCE.
"Now beside the river's bank we see Death impending
But, of course, heaven's force gave a happy ending

(PRUDENCE exits, backwards, with GILLIAN, facing forward, moving sideways. Exeunt Left of screen. Simultaneously POLLY moving backwards, exits Right of screen.)

KENDALL. *(Enters Right of screen, facing forwards, walking sideways, distributing fish.)*
"So Evil is defeated and the world's a better place
And as for me well obviously I'm in a state of Grace
Free of vice and very nice, I'm Pure and Good and True
(Deliberately.) Since I'm a saint and most of you ain't, I'll tell you what to do. *(KENDALL exits Left of screen. From behind the screen, hisses.)* Mother, you're on again!
POLLY. *(From behind the screen.)* Already?
KENDALL. *(From behind the screen.)* Get out there!
POLLY. *(Erupts, apparently pushed even harder than before, from Right of screen. It takes her a second to orientate herself. Comes to Center. POLLY is ill.)*
"Happy endings not withstanding, I must play my part
Saint or sinner, looser, winner someone must depart
Death will not be defeated not cheated of her prey

Stay with me ....
(Pause. We have no idea what POLLY is thinking or feeling because she is wearing the blank, featureless white cipher of a mask. Starts again.)

Death will not be defeated nor cheated of her prey
Stay with me ... and you will see ....

(Pause. She is alone on stage, in black, expressionless.)

JESSICA. *(Face only. Left of screen, prompting quietly.)* Stay with me and you will see Death always knows the way.
POLLY.
"Stay with me ... and you will see ... Death....
GILLIAN. *(Face only, prompting louder.)* and you will see Death always knows the way.
POLLY.
"Stay with me ...
(JESSICA gasps. The scythe shaft serving as support, POLLY sinks to her knees.) I ... I feel a little dizzy.

(ALL come out from behind the screen; harp, lance, and axe are left behind.)

JESSICA. Polly!
KENDALL. *(Simultaneously.)* Mother! *(JESSICA, KENDALL, and LACEY all rush to POLLY. Because of the "horse" JESSICA is edged out. KENDALL and LACEY, each having taken one of POLLY's arms and raised her are turning toward the kitchen Incidentally, the rain has apparently stopped because the living room is brightening and coming back into our view.)* Mother, come and sit down.
JESSICA, Give her some water.
GILLIAN. Give her some brandy.
KENDALL. *(As they go.)* Did you take your medicine?

LACEY. I've got the door.
KENDALL. Take it slowly.
JESSICA. *(As they exit.)* Call a doctor.

(KENDALL, LACEY, and POLLY have exited to the kitchen.)

GILLIAN. You can't get through to a doctor nowadays.
PRUDENCE. Do we need an ambulance then? Or fire-rescue, they come.
GILLIAN. *(Sincerely.)* I'll pay for a private doctor if we can get one. I'd do anything. I'd give up drinking. I'd give up smoking. Anything.
JESSICA. I wish I weren't wearing this thing. It doesn't help; it gets in the way. *(Tense.)* Gillian, do something.
GILLIAN. *(For once at a loss.)* I don't know what to do.
PRUDENCE. A cold compress is always good.
JESSICA. For what?
PRUDENCE. Most everything, I think.

(The phone rings. GILLIAN turns and crosses to it. It stops ringing as she gets there.)

GILLIAN. *(On phone.)* Hello, ... *(Listens momentarily.)* Oh, sorry. *(Hangs up.)* They got it already.
JESSICA. Who?
GILLIAN. Polly. And it sounded like that Wilson woman. I don't know what that means.
JESSICA. Well, it means she's not dead.
GILLIAN. *(Releasing tension.)* Dead!? What idiot thought she was going to be dead?
JESSICA. You did. And for a moment there ... I did.
GILLIAN. You are so stupid.
JESSICA. I am not stupid. You just say mean things because you

hate me. You've always hated me. *(Sensing her big scene.)* You resent me and we all know why. You're consumed with jealousy. Gillian, I didn't take Henry away from you. Henry left you and came to me. I was just there and he found me irresistible. I was, let's face it, lovely. *(To PRUDENCE.)* Of course, I was younger then. *(Beat.)* And I wasn't dressed as a horse. *(To GILLIAN.)* You have every right to hate me. Because my gain is your loss. *(Inspired.)* And Henry's gain is the theater's loss. And that's why she hates me.
 PRUDENCE. She likes you.
 JESSICA. *(Oblivious.)* And I don't hate you for hating me.
 PRUDENCE. She likes you.
 JESSICA. *(It registers.)* Oh. Well, where's the fun in that? *(Hopefully to GILLIAN.)* Did I ruin your life? I did, didn't I? I ruined your life.
 GILLIAN. Nonsense. I've everything I've ever wanted. I think.
 PRUDENCE. *(To JESSICA.)* It wasn't like that, really. Gillian planned ...
 GILLIAN. *(Cutting off, fast.)* Use prudence, Prudence.
 PRUDENCE. Oh, sorry.

(There is a great anguished cry "Noooo!" from KENDALL off-stage. ALL turn toward kitchen. The cry repeats "Noooo!")

 JESSICA. Oh, my God!

(KENDALL enters from the kitchen. She is racked with great heaving sobs. Between which, as she comes Center.)

 KENDALL. It's over!
 GILLIAN. *(Sinks onto hassock. Softly.)* Oh, Polly.
 KENDALL. It's all over.

(LACEY rushes in from the kitchen to KENDALL.)

LACEY. It's all right.

KENDALL. No! It's not all right. *(Sob.)* What will I do now?

LACEY. It'll be all right.

KENDALL. No, it won't. She's sold the house!

GILLIAN. *(Rising.)* What?

KENDALL. She's sold the house.

(KENDALL sobs.)

GILLIAN. Well, God bless her.

JESSICA. *(Who has crossed to kitchen door during the above.)* Polly!

POLLY. *(Enters from the kitchen without her mask.)* I'm sorry. I'm so sorry. I should have eaten breakfast. But I've had some brandy and some Twinkies and I feel much, much better.

PRUDENCE. We were so worried.

GILLIAN. *(Still worried.)* Jessica? Jessica, did I just give up smoking?

JESSICA. Don't worry, Gillian, you're not that well-connected.

KENDALL. But where will I go? What will I do?

GILLIAN. Why does "get a job" spring to my lips?

JESSICA. Lacey needs a roommate.

KENDALL. *(To LACEY.)* Do you believe in sisterhood?

LACEY. No, I don't. But I do believe in rent.

KENDALL. I was going to use the house to do good.

POLLY. *(Crossing to comfort her.)* Oh, Kendall, don't be good, dear. It's much too hard. Good is for saints. Just be forgiving and polite, you'll do a lot less harm.

(KENDALL stifled sob.)

JESSICA. Well, I've certainly learned an important lesson that we should all keep in mind. If you think you want to go, go ahead and go before you climb into a horse costume.

POLLY. *(Front and Center.)* Now about this clock. It's supposed to be fun. So all together.

> One o'clock
>> Two o'clock
>>> Three o'clock chime
>>> Glockenspiel girls let's tell the time

(They ALL join her, except KENDALL.)

ALL (except KENDALL).
> One o'clock
>> Two o'clock
>>> . Night or day
>>> Glockenspiel girls come out to play.

(POLLY goes back and brings KENDALL up to join them. They are an oddly costumed chorus line.)

ALL.
> One o'clock
>> Two o'clock
>>> Fast not slow
>>> Glockenspiel girls let's go, go, go!

(Curtain.)

END OF PLAY

PROPERTY LIST

ACT I

Mounted fish — PRESET
5 ashtrays, dust cloth — POLLY
Drinks tray, alcoholic — POLLY
Watch — POLLY
Water sports bottle —LACEY
Drinks tray, non-alcoholic — KENDALL
Photos — POLLY
Folder of loose papers —PRUDENCE
Handbag with cigarettes and non-functioning lighter —GILLIAN
Mop/Squeegee — POLLY
Basket of plastic flowers — POLLY
Dustpan —POLLY
Long-handled feather duster — POLLY
Laundry bag, full — POLLY
Accordion or concertina — POLLY

ACT II

Gong — PRESET
Kitchen stool — PRESET
Part of costume, not practical — PRESET
Carpet/rug — PRESET
Sewing basket/container — PRESET
Pennant, small — JESSICA
Basket of non-realistic fish, color matches flowers — POLLY
Hideous Halloween mask, not worn — POLLY
Paper or plastic plate with food — PRUDENCE
Handheld non-practical music player, cardboard, one per each performance — JESSICA

COSTUMES

POLLY (sixty-ish): Sweat pants, large faded Hawaiian shirt; similarly casual in Act II.

KENDALL (thirty-ish): Smart street clothes.

LACEY (late twenties): Sporty casual; similar but sexier in Act II.

JESSICA (fifty-ish): Lederhosen (like the Clock Costumes can be rented), high heels; expensively casual in Act II.

GILLIAN (early fifties): Crisp, austere street clothes; similarly in Act II.

PRUDENCE (early twenties): Maternity clothes.

(All ages are very approximate and relative; may be varied. Also because this is Florida the ladies may be from anywhere and have any backgrounds and accents. There is no need for any Florida or "beach" effect in the play.)

CLOCK COSTUMES

POLLY (Death): Black hooded monk's robe. Scythe. Featureless, colorless mask (these are made of plastic and if necessary the lover part can be cut away to free the mouth and jaw, making a half-mask.

KENDALL (Saint Ermintrude): Nun's habit, but not black—black is reserved for Death. Basket of fish, matches flowers. Possibly from beneath the wimple stick the ends of yellow braids that match the other yellow braids.

LACEY (Maiden Ermintrude): Dirndl, which is a traditional German folk costume. Or a similar pretty peasant costume. Braids. Basket of flowers.

PRUDENCE (Angel): Traditional angel with halo and large wings.

Harp—need be neither realistic nor practical. Knee pads under costume for crawling.

GILLIAN (Pagan Queen): Traditional Viking Queen (Brunehilde). Braids. Helmet. Battle-axe.

   (Saint in Sack): Gillian without her helmet, her yellow braids matching the other braids. The sack, which can be very simple, should have holes cut for the feet. There should be enough fabric so that its droop mostly conceals the feet. There should also be enough fabric so that the actor can raise and lower the sack from inside to cover her face—this gives the effect of popping up and down without the actor having to stoop.

KENDALL (Knight on horseback): Ideally and most effectively, a costume in which the actor walks beneath the caparison (skirting) of the horse and the knight's "legs" are part of the costume. However, the play will also work with a version of a hobby horse. Lance with huge, really huge banner.

(Although angels are generally in white, dirndls contain a lot of white, and nun's habits are often white, try and vary this. The nun could be pale blue, the angel gold. The overall effect for the clock figures is to be brightly, theatrically colorful. This is toy theater. The recent increase in Party and Costume/Halloween shops make these costumes and props fairly easy to find. Also, on the Internet are many, many costume outlets and sites for Renaissance and Medieval Fairs and Festivals.)

STAGING NOTES

STAGE RIGHT	STAGE LEFT
POLLY/Death (facing S Left)	JESSICA/Knight on horseback (facing S Right)
KENDALL/Maiden Ermintrude (facing Front)	PRUDENCE/Angel (facing S Right)
LACEY/Ermintrude the Nun (facing Front)	GILLIAN/Gundra (facing S Right)
GILLIAN/Ermintrude in sack (facing Front)	

In ACT II, Lacey and Kendall have switched roles. Gillian is in the sack only in Act II.

The movements should be mechanical, clockwork and specific, but once established need not be slavishly adhered to. Similarly the direction-faced can be loosened during the last clock sequence.

Flowers and Fish—The baskets should be suspended around the neck. The movement is one hand holding a flower (or fish) extends fully to the side, stops, and returns to basket. The other hand then mirrors on the other side; not simultaneously. Always facing front.

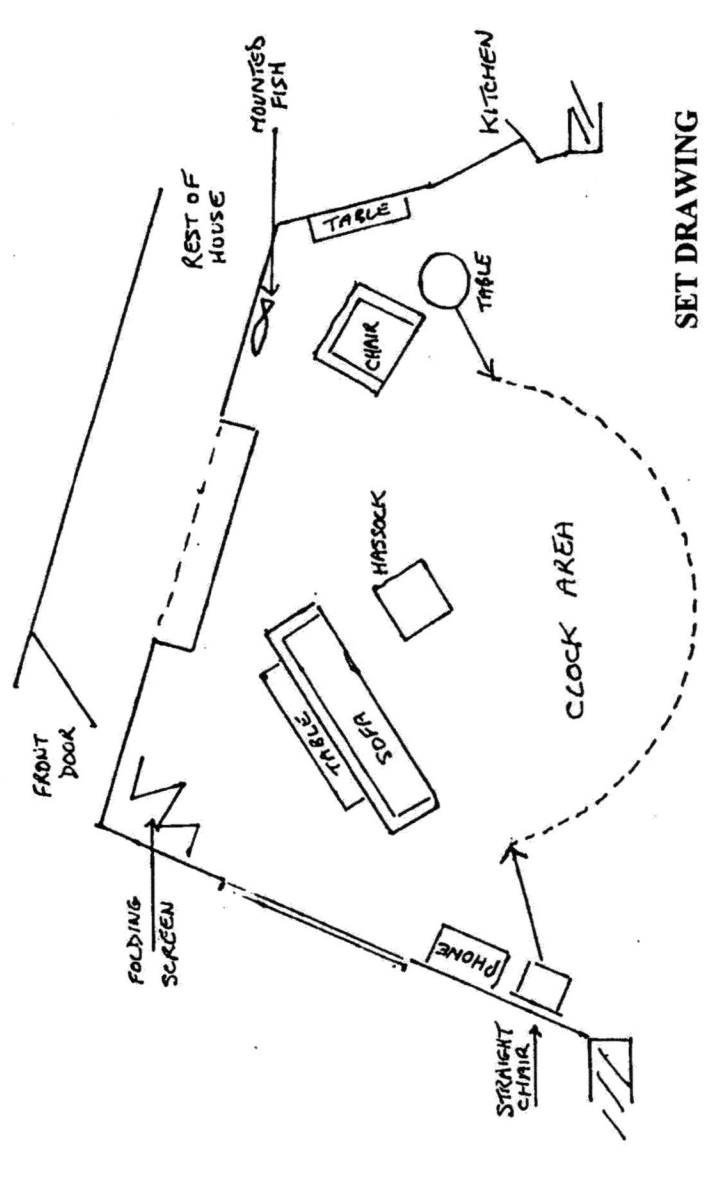

SET DRAWING

CAPTIVE
Jan Buttram

Comedy / 2m, 1f / Interior

A hilarious take on a father/daughter relationship, this off beat comedy combines foreign intrigue with down home philosophy. Sally Pound flees a bad marriage in New York and arrives at her parent's home in Texas hoping to borrow money from her brother to pay a debt to gangsters incurred by her husband. Her elderly parents are supposed to be vacationing in Israel, but she is greeted with a shotgun aimed by her irascible father who has been left home because of a minor car accident and is not at all happy to see her. When a news report indicates that Sally's mother may have been taken captive in the Middle East, Sally's hard-nosed brother insists that she keep father home until they receive definite word, and only then will he loan Sally the money. Sally fails to keep father in the dark, and he plans a rescue while she finds she is increasingly unable to skirt the painful truths of her life. The ornery father and his loveable but slightly-dysfunctional daughter come to a meeting of hearts and minds and solve both their problems.

OTHER TITLES AVAILABLE FROM SAMUEL FRENCH

COCKEYED
William Missouri Downs

Comedy / 3m, 1f / Unit Set
Phil, an average nice guy, is madly in love with the beautiful Sophia. The only problem is that she's unaware of his existence. He tries to introduce himself but she looks right through him. When Phil discovers Sophia has a glass eye, he thinks that might be the problem, but soon realizes that she really can't see him. Perhaps he is caught in a philosophical hyperspace or dualistic reality or perhaps beautiful women are just unaware of nice guys. Armed only with a B.A. in philosophy, Phil sets out to prove his existence and win Sophia's heart. This fast moving farce is the winner of the HotCity Theatre's GreenHouse New Play Festival. The St. Louis Post-Dispatch called Cockeyed a clever romantic comedy, Talkin' Broadway called it "hilarious," while Playback Magazine said that it was "fresh and invigorating."

Winner!
of the HotCity Theatre GreenHouse New Play Festival

"Rocking with laughter...hilarious...polished and engaging work draws heavily on the age-old conventions of farce: improbable situations, exaggerated characters, amazing coincidences, absurd misunderstandings, people hiding in closets and barely missing each other as they run in and out of doors...full of comic momentum as Cockeyed hurtles toward its conclusion."
–Talkin' Broadway

TAKE HER, SHE'S MINE

Phoebe and Henry Ephron

Comedy / 11m, 6f / Various Sets

Art Carney and Phyllis Thaxter played the Broadway roles of parents of two typical American girls enroute to college. The story is based on the wild and wooly experiences the authors had with their daughters, Nora Ephron and Delia Ephron, themselves now well known writers. The phases of a girl's life are cause for enjoyment except to fearful fathers. Through the first two years, the authors tell us, college girls are frightfully sophisticated about all departments of human life. Then they pass into the "liberal" period of causes and humanitarianism, and some into the intellectual lethargy of beatniksville. Finally, they start to think seriously of their lives as grown ups. It's an experience in growing up, as much for the parents as for the girls.

"A warming comedy. A delightful play about parents vs kids. It's loaded with laughs. It's going to be a smash hit."
– *New York Mirror*

OTHER TITLES AVAILABLE FROM SAMUEL FRENCH

THE DECORATOR
Donald Churchill

Comedy / 1m, 2f / Interior

Marcia returns to her flat to find it has not been painted as she arranged. A part time painter who is filling in for an ill colleague is just beginning the work when the wife of the man with whom Marcia is having an affair arrives to tell all to Marcia's husband. Marcia hires the painter, a part-time actor, to impersonate her husband at the confrontation. Hilarity is piled upon hilarity as the painter, who takes his acting very seriously, portrays the absent husband. The wronged wife decides that the best revenge is to sleep with Marcia's husband, an ecstatic experience for them both. When Marcia learns that the painter/actor has slept with her rival, she demands the opportunity to show him what really good sex is.

"Irresistible."
– London Daily Telegraph

"This play will leave you rolling in the aisles....
I all but fell from my seat laughing."
– London Star

OTHER TITLES AVAILABLE FROM SAMUEL FRENCH

THREE YEARS FROM "THIRTY"
Mike O'Malley

Dramatic Comedy / 4m, 3f / Unit set

This funny, poignant story of a group of 27-year-olds who have known each other since college sold out during its limited run at New York City's Sanford Meisner Theater. Jessica Titus, a frustrated actress living in Boston, has become distraught over local job opportunities and she is feeling trapped in her long standing relationship with her boyfriend Tom. She suddenly decides to pursue her dreams in New York City. Unbeknownst to her, Tom plans to propose on the evening she has chosen to leave him. The ensuing conflict ripples through their lives and the lives of their roommates and friends, leaving all of them to reconsider their careers, the paths of their souls and the questions, demands and definition of commitment.